One Strong Girl

Surviving The Unimaginable:
A Mother's Memoir

S. Lesley Buxton

Pottersfield Press, Lawrencetown Beach, Nova Scotia, Canada

Library and Archives Canada Cataloguing in Publication

Buxton, S. Lesley, 1965-, author
        One strong girl : surviving the unimaginable : a mother's memoir / S. Lesley Buxton.
Issued in print and electronic formats.
ISBN 978-1-988286-64-8 (softcover).--ISBN 978-1-988286-65-5 (PDF)
        1. Buxton, S. Lesley, 1965-. 2. Parents of terminally ill children--Canada--Biography.
3. Mothers and daughters. 4. Buxton Taylor, India. 5. Spinal muscular atrophy--Patients--
Canada--Biography. 6. Nervous system--Degeneration--Patients--Canada--Biography.
7. Myoclonus. 8. Terminally ill children--Family relationships. 9. Children--Death. I. Title.
RC365.B89 2018   616.8'047092   C2018-903411-4
                                                  C2018-903412-2

Cover image: Moorea Hum; Photo: Lesley Buxton

Cover design: Gail LeBlanc from a design by Mark Taylor

Pottersfield Press gratefully acknowledges the financial support of the Government of Canada through the Canada Book Fund for our publishing activities. We also acknowledge the support of the Canada Council for the Arts and the Province of Nova Scotia which has assisted us to develop and promote our creative industries for the benefit of all Nova Scotians.

Pottersfield Press
248 Leslie Road
East Lawrencetown, Nova Scotia, Canada, B2Z 1T4
Website: www.PottersfieldPress.com
To order, phone 1-800-NIMBUS9 (1-800-646-2879) www.nimbus.ca

Printed in Canada

RECYCLED
Paper made from recycled material
FSC® C103567

Pottersfield Press is committed to preserving the environment and the appropriate harvesting of trees and has printed this book on Forest Stewardship Council® certified paper.

For Mark and India, my little family

... you work,
so hard, all day
To be like other girls.
— Joss Hill Whedon
"Something To Sing About"

Contents

1

Spiriting Away

Kamikakushi (literally "hidden by Kami") means "spirited away." In Japanese legend it's believed if you chase after a person stolen by the Gods, you'll confront the anger of the spirits. Even in modern Japan, when children go missing, they are said to be the victims of Kamikakushi.

– Japanese Folklore

The Air Nippon flight from Vancouver to Tokyo is packed. Our fellow passengers are either Japanese Canadians or Japanese tourists returning home. The few passengers of European descent – including my husband Mark and me – seemed pasty, gawky, and huge in comparison. Over the next sixty days, this is a feeling I will have to get used to. No matter where I go I will feel like a giant, my hands and feet oversized and mannish. We've been in the air an hour or so. Flying through time into the next day.

The flight attendants slowly make their way down the aisles with the drink carts. They remind me of grown-up versions of the characters in the favourite anime shows of my recently deceased daughter, India, but instead of high school uniforms they wear dark skirts and light blouses with tidy well-pressed aprons. They all seem to wear the same scarlet lipstick. They smile at each other, chatting loudly as they hand out cans of Kirin, Asahi, and the occasional good Scotch. I like the fact my fellow travellers seem to enjoy alcohol as much as I do.

I wonder what India would be drinking if she were with us. She was sixteen when she died so we never got the chance to have a drink together. But I imagine if she were here, I might order her a glass of champagne to toast our trip.

I'm on my way to a country that embraces conformity. Already I'm uncomfortable with this. It reminds me of all my years at boarding school wearing that dreadful itchy kilt. I never liked matching the other girls. Always tried to bring some individuality to my uniform by wearing bangles or fingerless lace gloves.

India would've hated wearing a uniform as well, though like most people who've never done it, she liked the idea of it.

Japan has never been my dream country. I know very little about it other than what my daughter has taught me. I never understood her fascination with it. I can't even remember when her obsession began. Was it that damn Tamagotchi she got when she was seven or eight? Hers was purple. The game was designed so the owner had to care for the Tamagotchi pet, feed it, look after it when it got sick. India's was always dying. Or maybe she fell in love with the photos my sister, Margaret, showed her from when she lived there, of all the teenage girls in their flowery kimonos tottering down the narrow streets of Kyoto in their white socks and wooden Geta sandals.

When we visited the epilepsy clinic at Sick Kids hospital in Toronto, India always insisted we visit the little Japanese boutique in Kensington Market where they sold the Harajuku fashion. She was so sick then, shaky and constantly on the verge of falling, and so tiny. She wore a size zero. She looked like a doe-eyed anime character. She even acted like one, one moment, placid and smiling, the next losing her temper. Her eyes were so manic I half-expected stars and X's to shoot from them like one of her favourite characters.

Mark and I would take turns following her through the shop as she admired animal hoodies, Steampunk black corseted dresses, skirts with crinolines, tiny veiled black hats, pastel Lolita dresses with puffy sleeves and aprons. We were afraid of her falling over, which she did frequently and without warning. There were so many accidents over the years. I've lost count of all her injuries.

India spent hours running the fabric through her fingers like some old European tailor trying to get the most for his money. She always had money too. From her grandmother or her great-aunt or from the allowance we were always forgetting to give her. Eventually she became friends with the Japanese woman who owned the store. She was so fond of India that she'd give us a break and follow her around. Of course, we couldn't relax. We'd sit outside the boutique, waiting nervously for the next disaster.

I pull out my carry-on bag, open it, and slide my hand into a red Chinese embroidered bag about the size of a Crown Royal whiskey bag. It holds the sixteen colourful glass beads, each containing a speck of Indy dust – this is what Mark and I have named her cremated remains.

In the end we will leave nine in Japan. Each bead is about the size of a shooting marble, the kind our daughter used to collect when she was in grade three or four. Some are perfectly round, others are doughnut shaped. Mark has strung them on a burgundy velvet ribbon. I'm terrified of losing them. The beads are made using a technique called lampworking. The colours are layered, the images made by manipulating glass pipes that look like coloured spaghetti.

Each Indy bead represents an aspect of who she was. There's a red one that looks like a tiny 1950s flying saucer, another that says "sing" with a musical note, one with a singing bird, a blue and silver bead that looks like the earth seen from space. There are small cracks inside the glass that remind me of firecrackers breaking through the night sky. When I run my hands over the beads I can feel these. This is the India dust. Lezlie Winemaker, the artist who made them, told me that when India's remains hit the fire they sizzled. "She's a feisty one. I can tell," she said.

When Lezlie phoned to tell me this, I was sitting in my living room listening to Annie Lennox sing "Love Song for a Vampire" and crying for my daughter. Lezlie had a way of calling whenever I was questioning how I'd carry on. As if she'd been talking to India who told her to call.

I'm not sure if it was Mark's or my idea that we'd go to Japan for India's birthday, but the minute it was suggested we both knew it was the right way to honour it. We had promised her long ago if she worked hard to get well we'd take her there. This was long before it ever occurred to us she might die. It's one of my major regrets we never took her. I wish we had.

Her birthday, May 24, was a busy time in the Quebec village where we once lived – cottagers returning to open up their properties, villagers on the river boating or drinking on some sunny patio celebrating the long Victoria Day weekend. I couldn't face the idea of seeing all that joy so I was glad to be heading to the other side of the world.

When we first thought of going to Japan, I thought we'd just smuggle India's ashes into the country, but later I became afraid that if we were found out they'd take them away from us. It was Margaret who inspired the idea of the beads. She'd met a glass-maker in Vancouver making beads for the bereaved. But this woman was expensive; she charged two hundred dollars a bead. This was way over our budget.

I never could stand the idea of burying India. The idea of her slowly decaying in the ground. I was troubled by horror film visions of her scratching at her coffin, her fingernails bleeding, raw and red as she tried to escape.

The minute we met Lezlie I knew she was the one. We'd

found her through friends who worked with wrought iron. She lived in Aurora, just outside Toronto.

When we entered her home, it was difficult to know where to look first. The walls were covered with glass dolls: queens in fine dresses, ladies in beaded dresses, goddesses with pointy breasts and wide hips, fairies with wire wings, naked women in bed with their lovers, even a glass menorah. My daughter would've been entranced.

I was at ease with Lezlie straight away. Sitting around her large dining room table while she made us tea, I felt unusually safe. I remember saying, "There's three Lesleys sitting here. Mark's middle name is Leslie too." She liked this and smiled broadly. For a while I allowed myself to imagine India's spirit was with us, zipping through the room, stopping to look at all the art.

I'm not sure if this really happened but I think I remember Lezlie saying, "India's here with us."

That day, as we headed away from Lezlie's house through the surrounding suburbs, past strip malls and car dealerships, I felt as if I was still talking to her. As if Lezlie was telling me she was going to look after my girl and not to be afraid. I was so deeply lost in this internal conversation I almost didn't hear Mark when he asked if I was hungry.

I touch the pendant hanging around my neck and feel the grooves where India's ash melds with the glass. Lezlie made me it as a special keepsake. It's light blue, the weight of a small rock, and features a girl with wild black hair. It has the feel of a Klimt painting. It's heavy around my neck. I keep tugging on it. Sometimes it makes me feel as if I'm choking.

Five hours into the flight, I've watched a Disney movie and a Japanese pop review of sorts. The last video featured a young Japanese female singer with long, drooping ponytails and braids tied in ribbons, her eyes smeared with yellow and green eye shadow. Her style of dress is half Goldie Hawn from the *Laugh-In* years, half Raggedy Anne doll. Even though I've no idea what she's singing about I enjoy it. I know India would watch it if she was here.

Mark sits by the window. I have the seat closest to the aisle. Usually I'm afraid of flying but I feel no fear. Part of this is that I no longer fear death. It's okay now. I don't mind going wherever my daughter is. Even if that means not existing at all. But I'm certain our flight won't crash or explode because we're on a mission. I close my eyes, try to sleep.

In the last years of India's illness I was always tired. I couldn't wait to sleep at night. I'd fall asleep the minute my head hit the pillow. I was aware that any moment my sleep could be interrupted; we never knew what the night would bring: hallucinations, seizures, some new terror I'd never imagined. Now sleep has become nothing but an escape. I still sleep deeply but often as I fall asleep I'm visited by cruel images of the past. I think about the last minutes of her life or her seizing on our sofa. In the early months after her death, the only way I could fall asleep was by clutching her favourite sock monkey in my arms and pretending it was her.

Five months after my daughter's death, I still understand little of this new way of living. I feel as though I've been plucked out of my old body and placed in another body, which has nothing to do with me. This new woman walks too slowly, struggles to catch her breath, and perpetually feels as if she's being watched.

When I was still an actor in my early twenties, I was in a show where I had to wear very high heels. I begged the costumer to give me a pair of court shoes but she wouldn't. I knew I'd fall in the heels. I practised walking in them but I never felt comfortable. Each time I went on stage, instead of trying to become the character I was playing, I was focused on staying upright. Eventually one night I walked on stage and I caught the edge of the rug under my heel and started to trip. Luckily the actor I was working with caught my hand

and pulled me up. I remember hearing a man in the front row gasp.

These days it feels as if I'm constantly on the cusp of falling. Experience has taught me I will survive the fall, but living on the edge like this is daunting. I want to go back to my old life with my daughter. Back to the world I understood. I don't know what to expect of Japan. I only know it's the best place for now.

Tokyo's Haneda airport is not as I expected. I've been conditioned to expect crowds but it doesn't seem any busier than Vancouver airport. We take an overhead skyway to the subway. It's about nine o'clock at night. I watch the city through the large windows. The landscape, with its layers of dark blue and reflecting lights, has a dream-like feel. We are surrounded by businessmen in dark suits of good quality. They study their phones and watches as if they're all involved in something terribly important. Our hotel is in the Ginza, the upmarket shopping area of Tokyo. We will spend two nights here and then we are off to Kyoto.

We arrive at our station finally and stagger through the gates with our luggage and carry-on bags, up the stairs, and onto the streets. Outside it's like a scene from the movie *Blade Runner*. Billboards flicker, crowds race across the street, and at every corner there's a games arcade with pounding electronic music. I feel like my head is on a swizzle stick. I look one way then the next. I'm completely disoriented. No idea where I'm supposed to go. I've lost my bearings – which direction is north? Which south?

Everything is a smear of light and sound. I look over at Mark. I can tell he's unsure as well. We know the hotel is close but we have no idea where. We head up the main street and hail a cab. The cab driver turns his car around the corner and we are at the hotel in less than three minutes. Though, now, twenty dollars poorer.

Later, after we've checked into our hotel, we find ourselves on the same street searching for food. In a shop about the size of my kitchen we find lots of choices – everything from Caesar salad to fried chicken. In the cooler I find a shelf filled with *onigiri*, triangles of cooked rice surrounded by seaweed, available with loads of different fillings. I know about these from watching India's favourite anime show, *Fruits Basket*. In the last months of her life, I used to lie in her bed and watch it with her. She'd howl with delight as the characters fell in and out of love.

Mostly I remember the theme song. She used to sing along with it when she could. We even considered playing it at her memorial.

Usually I was too worried to follow the plot of the show. Mostly I concentrated on holding her hand. It was the same shape as my own, only her fingers were longer and more elegant. Her hands were always warm and soft.

In those last months, I was constantly trying to get as physically close to her as I could. It depended on her mood whether she'd let me or not. Sometimes, though, I'd get sucked into the episode and begin asking India questions, which would annoy her. I never could understand why. She'd watched each episode at least ten times.

I pick a pork and a vegetable *onigiri*. Mark orders some *gyoza*, Japanese pork dumplings. We each buy a can of beer. We need to sleep. The next day will be busy. It's the beginning of our pilgrimage.

Hibiya Koen Park is surrounded by a heavy grey wall that looks like it belongs around a medieval fortress. It feels as if Mark and I are standing inside some strange stone womb. I'm freezing. The back of my dress is soaked from the wind and the rain. I'm sheltered in a wooden gazebo with a green roof with a large ginger cat that looks as if it belongs in a fairy tale, while Mark explores an outcropping at the edge of the pond.

Except for those scurrying through, we are the only people in the park. We are too late for the cherry blossoms but the park is still beautiful. There are plants with bell-shaped red petals, ornamental grasses, and oddly shaped pine trees right out of a Dr. Seuss book. Where Mark is standing looks like the miniature sculpted landscape around my mother's bonsai tree.

"I think we should put a bead here," Mark says. "India would like it." He points to a patch of earth beneath a shrub with fuchsia flowers near the pond.

I nod in agreement, watch as he presses the bead just under the surface of the earth. This is the second bead. The first was placed in Johnny Cash's tour bus at the Rock and Roll Hall of Fame in Cleveland, Ohio, in the beginning of May. India was a huge fan. She'd watched the film *Walk the Line* many times, and knew all the words to his songs.

The bead is robin's egg blue on the inside and clear glass on the outside. On the blue glass there are black and white circles placed randomly around the bead. The Indy dust has caused the clear glass to crack so it looks like a shard of sunlight peeking from behind a cloud.

I used to let myself pretend that India loved Japan so much because in another life she had lived here. Silly, really. But here in the park, remembering her, I allow this thought to cross my mind again. I let myself think of her as a little Japanese girl running along the pathway, scurrying towards the water and dragging her hand through it.

In the end I decided it doesn't really matter if it's real or not. It comforts me.

The next bead we take to the Harajuku district. This area is known for being the height of Japanese youth fashion.

On Saturdays young people hang around the subway station showing off their newest look. This is the area I know India would've been desperate to see.

The streets in this area are wide and we aren't sure where to go. It's still raining and I'm still cold. All around us, young people pass us, carrying shopping bags filled with the latest fashions. We reach a busy intersection and decide to go into what looks like a mall. There's a flag over the entrance with a picture of three Disney princesses. We ride the escalator up to the first floor. Unlike malls in Canada, there are many levels but with very little floor space.

On the first floor there's a big canopy with a fancy-looking throne of sorts. From what I can figure this is where Disney enthusiasts can have their photos taken as a princess. But it isn't little kids hanging around but teenage girls. This area is enclosed by racks of Disney princess T-shirts and other paraphernalia. If India was here she'd definitely want to have her photo taken.

Before she got really sick but was still falling unexpectedly, I took her to an overnight arts camp with me where I was teaching drama. She took art. She drew all the time before she lost control of her hands. One night her cabin gave a performance of the song "Under the Sea" from *The Little Mermaid*. I remember watching her play Sebastian, the lobster. She was completely involved, leaping about the stage and fully engaged in the character while I sat there, gripping my seat, praying she wouldn't fall.

Looking back, it's hard to grasp that this girl was dying. At the time we thought she had absence seizures: a kind of epileptic seizure characterized by a blank stare that lasts a few seconds. They generally cause no long-term problems, but in India's case they seemed to be causing her to fall down without warning. Mark and I were constantly on guard, ready to catch her. We were still optimistic that eventually she'd get better. Sometimes I wish I'd known. If I'd known I'd have taken her to Japan. I would've taken her anywhere. At other times I'm thankful that I had no inkling. During the six months I did know, there were many times I had to turn away from her so she wouldn't see me crying. I was so terrified that sometimes just watching her sleep made me feel like I'd throw up.

On the top floor of the mall, Mark and I have a coffee while we make a plan. It's then that we spy it, the little veranda café, decorated with pictures of Disney princesses, empty and abandoned to the rain.

We finish our coffees and go outside. The courtyard is tiled and skirted by flowers and bushes. In the centre is a circular bar decorated with bouquets of flowers, flags with Disney emblems, and portraits of the princesses etched in plastic. I expect the courtyard is usually teaming with groups of girls. There's music playing from a speaker I can't locate. As if to confirm any reservations about whether this is a good place for a bead, it's playing India's song from *The Little Mermaid*.

The bead we leave here has a glowing pink centre. It looks like a prop from a play or something magical from Harry Potter. Like all the other beads, it is just the next one on the string but it's beautifully suited to its surroundings. I can't help hoping that once the warm weather returns some little Japanese girl will find it and keep it as a special treasure. I like the idea of the beads being found. This means India keeps travelling and having adventures. I want her to go everywhere. This was her dream.

I try not to feel sad as we plant the bead but it's hard. I know it's the right thing to do, that she belongs here in the country that tantalized her imagination for so many years. If she were alive I'd be encouraging her to travel here, but even so it's not easy to part with even the tiniest speck of her. When she was a toddler I used to tease her and say, "You're going to live with your mummy forever, right?"

Back then she'd smile and jump into my arms. "Yes, Mummy, yes."

Later when she was a teenager, I'd jokingly say this. Of course, by then she was tired of my game and would scowl and tell me I was crazy.

It seems far-fetched but I feel as if India knows we are doing this. Just in the day we've been here I already feel as if I'm understanding her attraction to Japan more and therefore learning more about her. All around me in Harajuku are young women dressed as she did. I can imagine her here, slipping her arm through a friend's as they stroll off towards the ramen house or over to some Steampunk boutique.

The next bead takes us far into the suburbs to a place known as Mitaka. Here the high-rises have been replaced by stucco cottages. There are bicycle paths. People walk their dogs and children gallop by. There's even a sculpture park, though sadly we have arrived too late in the afternoon to enjoy it.

We have come here because it's the home of the Ghibli museum, created by India's favourite director, Hayao Miyazaki. For years, she was a devoted fan, saving her money to buy his films. India's favourites were *Spirited Away, My Neighbor Totoro, Howl's Moving Castle, Kiki's Delivery Service,* and *Ponyo*.

She first saw *Kiki's Delivery Service* when she was about eight. It was in Japanese with subtitles and she watched it completely mesmerized. I'm not a big fan of animation, but there's a lot to admire about Miyazaki's stories. The main character is always a smart independent girl, and though she might have a friend who's a boy, there's never a romance; instead there's a friendship. Miyazaki is a Japanese legend. In 2012, he was named a Person of Cultural Merit by the Japanese government. He's also known and loved throughout the world.

We know the museum will be closed for renovations. We found this out shortly after we booked our tickets.

Nonetheless we are determined to place a bead here in India's honour.

When we reach the museum we find a large yellow stucco building enclosed by trees, and a fence with metal bars. The gate is iron and decorated with a coat of arms featuring characters from one of his most loved movies, *My Neighbor Totoro*. It looks like the entranceway to a Spanish count's villa. Looking through the bars of the gate, I spot a giant Totoro. India would've squealed with delight.

We circle the museum several times trying to figure out how we will get the bead on the grounds. I imagine throwing it over the fence and letting fate do the rest. But Mark's not keen on doing that. He's considering climbing over the fence when we see someone approach the gate.

I say "someone" as we promised to keep the identity of our helper a secret as part of the deal. All I can say is that Mark and I introduced ourselves to this person, who luckily spoke very good English, and told them our story. After taking some time to consider the meaning of what we were asking, they agreed. Our helper even sent us a photo of where the bead is laid to rest. I will always be grateful to this person, and that they came by when they did.

Kyoto is the Japan of India's imagination: groups of young women in kimonos wander through the streets of the old town; temples are tucked in next to market stalls, tea rooms, and Starbucks. There are delicate streams with half-moon bridges leading to little paths to the river. It is the Japan of *Memoirs of a Geisha*. Teenagers in school uniforms pass us by, waving and shouting hello. Some even stop to ask us where we come from or to take our photos. One asks if he can interview us for his English class.

The first night we are here, we stumble upon the Yasaka Shrine as the sun is going down and the temple's lights are slowly coming on. We follow the steps up to the orange gateway, not knowing at all what to expect. From there, we follow the red spirit houses along a stone pathway. We have entered India's world, the world she learned about in Miyazaki's movie *Spirited Away*. It's the tale of an angry ten-year-old girl, whose greedy parents are turned into pigs. She is forced to live in the realm of spirits under the command of an evil witch. The girl's new world is filled with phantoms, spirits, and ghosts. Standing here at the shrine, it's easy to see where Miyazaki got his inspiration. If India was with us, she'd be running up to the spirit houses and peeking into them.

The Shinto believe in Kami: spirits of sorts that are parts of nature, animals, evolutionary forces, or the spirits of the deceased – although, according to my reading, a spirit is really too simplistic a description. They believe heroes or royalty like great emperors become Kami. The Kami are very close to being human and answer prayers. Strangely I feel a certain reassurance in this. Since my daughter's death I frequently invoke her name when I'm scared. The Shinto, according to a BBC website I found, believe there are millions and millions of Kami in Japan. Some are evil and some are good. They aren't gods or angels in the way we Westerners think of them. Nor are they perfect. They can be mischievous like a sixteen-year-old girl.

After India died, a lot of people told me they believed she had something special, that they felt she'd been brought into the world to show us how to be good. I remember shuddering when an acquaintance of mine called her *a force for good*. Though I knew the intention was meant kindly, I couldn't help feeling they'd missed the significance of my loss. I wasn't mourning a saint. I was mourning the little girl who teased me, snuck out of bed and hid on the stairway, spying while my friends and I knitted and drank wine in the living room. Why did they have to make her into something more than what she was?

I had trouble with the concept that she was born for a purpose. This alluded to some sort of Christ-like being. It hurt me to think of her that way. It made me feel raw and angry. But I seldom said anything. I didn't want my daughter immortalized as a saint; I wanted her remembered as the person she was, faults and all.

The well-known Kami of the Shinto have names and legends. Though India wasn't famous I can see her as one, a higher expression of life energy. Even when she was dying she grasped life's power, her crooked wide smile, ferocious as she joked with me. The atmosphere at this temple only enhances my feeling of weightlessness. For months now, I've felt as if I was just moving through life. I don't want to make it sound like I'm sleepwalking because I'm aware of what I'm doing. It's more as if I'm stuck in some sort of buoyant, misty layer of the world suspended between the living and the dead. My life seems less concrete. I know I'm alive because I see myself doing things. I'm conscious of getting dressed, eating breakfast, walking down the street, but I can't seem to grab hold of the notion that it's all real.

Mark takes a photo of me with the bead. Then we leave a bead next to one of the red spirit houses. We're cataloguing as we go, hoping to collect all the images into something meaningful upon our return. We're hungry and thirsty. It's time to wander away from the temple and into the world again.

We will leave six beads in Kyoto. Two will stay in the Arashiyama district, the first at the famous bamboo forest. Another will be imbedded in a tiny patch of green between two crumbling grey Buddhas sitting outside the Adashino Nenbutsu-ji Temple, known for its thousands of stone Buddha statues, which have stood mourning the dead since the Heian period, over eight hundred years ago. There's a certain justice in this. After all, this is where the poor once brought the bodies of their loved ones and laid them to rest, without any markers.

On what would've been India's seventeenth birthday, almost seven months after her death, we go to the Kyoto International Manga Museum. We know as soon as we walk into the museum India would've spent hours here. It isn't like a museum at all really. It's more of a library, the walls heavy with bookshelves filled with every kind of Manga available. People of all ages sit on benches reading, curled in a corner, or lie outside under the sun, books stretched in front of them.

It's a funny day. I wonder if I didn't know the date if I'd instinctually feel sad. We have no rites for mothers whose children die. I don't know how to feel about the day or how to act. I can keenly remember every detail of her birth – on her birthday I used to torture India with the lurid details. Now these memories prick at me like the head of a pin lodged in my skin, just under my ribs. I want to tell people how happy I was to meet her but who wants to hear? It seems somehow wrong to talk about my dead daughter's birth. I worry that it will embarrass people or that they will view me as damaged goods and feel sorry for me.

We decide to place a bead inside a book but we have a hard time finding one that feels right. We pick up books, put them back, unsure she'd like them. Finally, we discover a selection of English titles and I find a Manga version of *Spirited Away*. It takes Mark a while to manage to hide the bead. There are so many people around and we don't want to get caught. Afterwards I feel depleted, as if I've just lost blood.

India's birthday is the only day we have Western food. Tired and grumpy, we reel into the local MacDonald's. I don't notice much different on the menu except they have green tea milkshakes and sundaes. When I bite into my Big Mac, though, it tastes different, as if the cheese has been flavoured with turmeric. This is a good analogy for my life. Everything looks the same but the flavour is all wrong.

Before we leave Kyoto, we throw a bead from Shijo Dori Bridge in the Kamo River. The scene is like the wood-cut print by Hiroshige, *Sudden Shower over Shin-Ōhashi bridge and Atake*. People march by, their umbrellas high and braced against the rain. It feels like we are making a wish but for what I don't know. There's nothing I want except my daughter and I've accepted that's impossible. So we both stand and look out at the river, each wondering where this bead will end up.

Back in Tokyo, we wander the old city. Here there are tea shops, market vendors, paper shops, and trendy clothing boutiques. We follow a path lined by cherry trees into the Yanaka Cemetery. The cemetery was once part of a Buddhist temple and the path is the old road to the temple. The road is well used. By accident we find the site of a burned-down five-storey pagoda. This is where we decide to leave our last Japanese bead. There's no particular reason except it feels right to leave this part of India here, not far from the site of ordinary graves and those belonging to shoguns.

The day is hot and we sit for a while. It's difficult to conceive that this area of the city represents what Tokyo once was, long before its modernizations. Most of old city is gone due to the great earthquake of 1923, fires, and the destruction of World War Two. Looking back, at that city and that day, I'm reminded of something India once said and that I wrote about in my blog: "Dad, my body is a lot like the country of India. Parts of it are at war like India and Pakistan. And it has a lot of earthquakes."

This seems true of Japan too, the dichotomy of skyscrapers and the ancient temples where the businessmen in their dark suits bow their heads to pray. It seems a good way to look at my life now. The before and after. The evidence of the other life imprinted on my skin as clearly as the way old Tokyo's customs are embedded in its future.

On our last evening in Tokyo, Mark and I wander the Ginza again. This time we don't worry about where we're going but instead let the crowds carry us through the streets. We end up in an arcade created by the overhead train bridge, and lined with small restaurants, bars, and food vendors. The air smells of grilled meats, gas, and beer. I find a crowded bar lined with high stools and tables and suggest to Mark we should eat. He agrees reluctantly. His tastes are more refined than mine and the place has the look of a student hangout. Groups of friends sit at the tables, drinking beer and chatting – most are dressed casually. It reminds me of the kind of place I might like at home. The atmosphere is strangely laid-back for here.

We take a seat, order beer, chicken Yakitori, and rice. As we wait for our food, I people watch. Imagine the conversations going on around me. I'm particularly intrigued by the group sitting directly in front of us. There are five of them: three men and two women.

Older looking than most of the patrons, they drink beer, chat, and laugh loudly. They aren't dressed in the typical manner either. Not one of them is wearing a suit. In fact, the oldest-looking man in the group is wearing a bright retro Hawaiian shirt. The other two men, though not as garishly dressed, are conspicuous in their casualness. They smile openly and don't seem confined by the politeness that seems to govern society here. The women too are more relaxed. The older woman, whose face is dominated by her wide dark eyes, takes large gulps of her beer and talks with her hands. The petite younger woman is more conservative in her attire, but I watch her smiling as she follows the group's chatter.

I wonder what they do for a living. Perhaps we have wandered accidentally into an artists' hangout?

I point the group out to Mark, who agrees they are definitely not typical. We take turns trying to guess what they do for a living. In the end we decide the man in the Hawaiian shirt is an art director and the others his employees at a graphic design studio. I know I should stop watching them. I worry that I'm being rude. Suddenly my thoughts are interrupted when one of the young men in the group turns to me and says in perfect English, "Where are you from?"

"Canada."

"Oh," he says. "My mother lives in Vancouver. Join us."

The group shifts around the table to make space for us. We make conversation despite the language barrier – only the young man and the young woman speak English, though everyone seems to understand most of what Mark and I say. The older woman, whose name I learn is Nana, attempts to speak to me, blushing as she trips over words. She is married to the man in the Hawaiian shirt. He's in the fashion industry and supplies Ugg boots to stores throughout Japan. It is his sixtieth birthday. There are two couples and our English-speaking young man. None of them have ever met before. Like us, they have simply stumbled into friendship.

This is unconventional for Japan but then again so is the group. Aside from the boot supplier, there's his stay-at-home wife, a pilot and an air hostess who are married, and our young English-speaker, a buyer for a big jean company.

Suddenly the young man, whose name I haven't yet learned, is gently touching my elbow. "We are going to the number two soul club in Tokyo. Come with us?" Without hesitation Mark and I agree.

As we are piling into a cab with the young man, there's a moment when I hesitate. In any other country I've travelled to, I might be reluctant to get into a cab with strangers who speak a language I don't understand. I push away my concern, though, and allow my sense of adventure to prevail. This is Japan, I tell myself, known for its lack of crime.

In the cab we learn we are going to the birthday boy's favourite place. He's a big fan of soul music and a regular at the establishment.

The club is on a narrow, dark, winding street. It reminds me of my years in London when my friends and I would go to after-hours clubs in Soho. Though unlike Soho, there are no neon signs flashing *Girls, Girls, Girls* or signs in the window advertising erotic massages. We enter an old brick building and climb up the stairs. The tiny club is dimly lit and tinged with red lights. A few couples sit at the back. The dance floor is empty despite the flood of disco lights and pulse of the music.

Mark and I are introduced to the number two soul DJ in Tokyo by the older man. He bows his head and we shake hands enthusiastically. I wonder how this man feels about being called the number two DJ. I'm not sure I would like it but he seems genuinely pleased. Someone in the party explains to me that it's a privilege to be in this club. It's one of those places where you have to be known to be allowed in.

Our group sits around a long table not far from the dance floor. The ladies pull out their phones and begin taking photos. The group poses are like scenes from one of India's anime shows. People make peace signs, smile, and hug. Nana repeats over and over to Mark, "Your wife, she is so cute." This makes me laugh. These women are stunning. In their company I feel like a sumo wrestler.

Everyone orders beer. Mark and I insist on paying but the group won't hear of it. We are guests in Japan, they tell us. This goes on, round after round, until Mark finally sneaks off to pay the waiter in private. They want to know everything about us but mostly why we are visiting Japan. We hesitate. For the first time in a very long time we are having fun. We are afraid our story will change everything.

As Mark tells them our story I watch as the young man quickly translates his words. I can see from the group's expression they are touched by our endeavour. I'm not sure who says it but one of the group tells us how honoured they are that India loved their homeland.

"My name is Ash," the young man says. "You came here with your daughter's ash and you met me. Fate."

"Yes, fate," I agree.

"To India," Ash says, raising his beer.

"To India," the group echoes, lifting their glasses.

"India has brought us all here together tonight," Ash says.

"Yes," I say, knowing that he is telling the truth.

2

Bridge

In our culture I think most people think of grief as sadness, and that's certainly part of it, a large part of it, but there's also this thorniness, these edges that come out.

– Anthony Rapp

I'm sitting in the dental chair reading *Hello!* magazine. The air smells of peppermint and burned metal. I shouldn't be scared. My dentist, Dr. W, has never hurt me. Rumour has it that he was once involved in a terrible snowmobile accident and forced to undergo months of dental surgery and ever since then he's been very careful with his patients. "This won't be long," he says, snapping on his gloves. "I'll just take it out today and when you get back from Cape Breton, we'll schedule you in for a bridge."

Fuck, I think to myself. *That'll cost a fortune.*

I open my mouth wide. He gives me three needles. I don't even wince. His assistant, an older woman who wears vibrantly coloured medical uniforms, places the dry vacuum in my mouth. I taste the latex of Dr. W's gloves as he tightens what feels like a ring around the remainder of my molar.

My broken molar feels like the tip of a craggy mountain. While Mark was driving me to the dentist, he had to shout at me because I couldn't stop touching it. India, who is ten years old, thought it was hilarious that I was in trouble and laughed at me as if I were the child and she was the adult.

"It'll be over in a snap," says Dr. W.

I close my eyes, open my mouth as far as I can. I feel the weight of his body as he leans into me and pulls the tooth with his pliers. Nothing. He struggles to get a better grip then yanks a second time. This continues for another half an hour.

I strain as I try my best to keep my mouth open. I'm on the verge of tears and I want my mother, who is miles away in Spain. The assistant pats my hand encouragingly every so often.

An hour passes. I'm on brink of getting out of the chair and leaving. The only thing that stops me is that we're supposed to be going on holiday with my friend Anita and I don't want a toothache to ruin our trip. The assistant is now holding my hand. Tears run down my face as Dr. W. pushes vigorously, using my shoulder as leverage. He pulls so hard that he grunts. I feel as though I've been punched in the face by a professional boxer.

Dr. W takes his hands from my mouth and exhales. "Got it. Got it."

I touch my wet face. My lips feel rubbery and hard.

"See," he says. "Damn tooth was stuck in your gum like a screw."

In the years to come, this day will stand out in my mind. A moment of foreshadowing, like a sentence in a mystery novel that predicts the murder to come. The gateway between the past and present.

I never got the bridge. From time to time, I rest my tongue in the empty space. I still can't stop touching it.

We're driving slowly from Ottawa to Cape Breton, making overnight stops at Rivière-du-Loup, Quebec, and Sackville,

New Brunswick. My jaw is swollen, my gums and mouth bruised. Anita and Mark share the driving. I could drive too but I only have my learner's and I don't have a lot of confidence. Plus I'm in pain. Every four hours, when the painkillers wear off, my mouth throbs.

We take turns sitting in the back with India, who listens to music or plays games on Mark's phone. Sometimes she sings with the radio or one of her CDs. Her voice is strong. Recently she's started voice lessons with a local jazz singer. It's the only class she's ever asked for. At her first lesson, the teacher stepped out of the classroom and called me over. "That girl can really sing," she tells me. "You were right."

Her teacher can't believe such a big voice belongs to such a young girl. Another teacher at the music school calls her The Little Diva. Her choir leader keeps telling me that she expects India to be a famous singer one day.

India is in that awkward stage of childhood – not quite a little kid anymore but not a teenager. She likes to walk with her friends to the corner store to buy candy but still wants to be tucked into her bed at night by her dad.

Her eyes are big and bold. They change from blue to green depending on what she's wearing. She has long dark lashes that tickle when she gives me butterfly kisses. Her complexion is different from mine, pale with an olive hue, more like Mark's.

Until recently she was short and stocky. Now she's long and lean. She's always climbing – trees, walls, ropes. She's good at it, except she's scared of heights so she has trouble getting down. Her long hair is golden-brown, but it's starting to go darker. She never brushes it. It's always matted at the nape of her neck.

She dresses like Pippi Longstocking – brightly coloured tights with striped shirts and mismatched socks. She likes her clothes to be soft. She rarely wears jeans.

We drive for hours. Occasionally India gets bored and says, "Are we there yet?" We tease her about this and repeat her words back to her. This makes her laugh. Her teeth are mismatched. She has what Mark calls a shark tooth as it sits in front of the rest and is sharp and jagged-looking.

Mark and I frequently talk about how eventually she will need braces. We worry about the expense. This is really all we have to worry about when it comes to India. We don't realize we are lucky. We think of ourselves as a happy family. In fact, I'm so certain of our happiness, I never worry about India. I'm sure nothing bad could ever happen to her.

In Cape Breton we stay at Anita's house in Main-à-Dieu. Writing this I'm struck by the name of the village. At the time I never gave it much thought. In English it means Hand of God. It sounds like a town in a Stephen King novel.

The quiet fishing village is known for its lobster fishing fleet. It reminds me of some remote Scottish island town. The kind of place where you walk into the pub and everyone turns around and glares at you. There is no pub, though, only a library, a fishing museum, and a small café. Often in the late afternoon, we walk down to the small beach at the end of the village to visit the sea. It's about fifteen minutes from the house.

At the beach, India runs around singing to herself as she collects pebbles and shells. Sometimes she paddles in the ocean. The water is cold even for her.

The walk back to the house is always laboured. India can't make it without falling on her knees. This only seems to happen in the late afternoon. During the morning and midday she's perfectly normal. Her knees are covered in Band-Aids, scabs, and cuts – scrapes on top of other scrapes. We can't figure out why this happening. In our frustration we sometimes lose our temper. She looks at us like we're crazy. She doesn't know why it's happening either.

At night after India is in bed, Mark, Anita, and I sit around the kitchen table, trying to work it out. Mark is afraid she might be having mini strokes or heart problems.

"She's just clumsy," I tell him. "My mother used to joke when I was growing up if there was only one thing in the room I'd fall over it. She's just getting used to her long legs. It'll stop."

When he pushes the matter further I get angry. I don't tell him this as I know it's irrational. After all, he's just worried about his child. By the end of the holiday two weeks later, there is no doubt in Mark's mind that there's something wrong. Now it's not just the falling that worries him. Sometimes he calls to India and she doesn't hear him. At other times he spots her staring into space, her legs twitching strangely. I don't see these things so I dismiss them.

Anita is spending the summer in Cape Breton so we take the train from Halifax home. On the train India races through the aisles with the other kids. They scurry about, laughing; they watch movies in the dining car. I catch Mark looking at her, searching for clues. His concern gnaws at me. When I see the way his eyes follow her, I want to shout, "Stop trying to find something wrong with her. She's fine."

Not long after our trip, my sister Margaret from Vancouver comes to visit us in Ottawa. India is thrilled to see her favourite auntie. Despite the summer humidity, the three of us venture downtown to the market area to visit the shops. India hangs on her aunt's arm, eager to be close to her.

In the afternoon we are walking down Dalhousie Street, near Mello's Café, when suddenly India falls face first into the sidewalk. She hits the ground so violently that she cracks her front tooth. I see it happen, but still I don't understand why. One moment she's upright and chatting to Margaret. The next, she's down, as if she's been struck on the head with a hammer.

Later I will tell my friends it's as if she dies for a moment then is suddenly reborn. Even later still, I will begin to understand why some cultures fear seizures – believe the victim is being enchanted by evil spirits.

Margaret and I rush to her. I pull her up, take her in my arms – hold her as tightly as I can. India is crying, shaking. Her knee is scraped, blood seeps down her leg.

"Are you okay, India? Are you okay?" Margaret stares at us. Her face strained with concern.

I pull my arms tightly around India. We are both scared.

The waitress from Mello's opens the door and calls to us. "Come in. I'll get her some water. That was a nasty fall."

We lead India into the café and take a seat in the booth. I sit with my arm around India's shoulder. I don't know what to do. India keeps rubbing her tooth with her finger. She's trembling. So am I.

"My tooth, Mummy. I'm not going to lose my tooth, am I?" She's worried because this is one of her new adult teeth.

"We'll take you to the dentist, don't worry. He'll fix it."

"Are you sure he can fix it?"

"Yes, yes, I'm sure he can."

Margaret and I bombard India with questions: "What happened? Did you trip? Did you feel funny? Were you hungry? Thirsty?"

"I don't know," India repeats over and over. "I don't know. I was just walking."

"Do you remember how you felt before you fell?" I have to force myself to keep my voice steady when I speak. I can tell there's an edge to my voice. I don't want India to know I'm worried. In the years to come, I will get a lot of practice in pretending not to be afraid. I will never master it.

"No, no. I don't know. I didn't feel anything, Mummy."

Margaret looks from India to me.

The waitress gives India a bowl of ice cream and a glass of water. She can't eat it. Her tooth hurts too much.

"Drink some water, India," Margaret says. "Maybe you were dehydrated."

India sips slowly at the water.

I order her a plate of fries. I'm worried that she fell because she was hungry. I don't know what to think. I tell myself there's a simple explanation: India's growing too fast, the humidity got to her, anything but face the fact she might be ill. I try to push those thoughts to the back of my mind.

The waitress brings the fries. India eats them, carefully avoiding her tooth. Margaret and I watch her, our eyes glued to her every gesture.

Mark takes India to his doctor at the drop-in clinic. He's too impatient to wait for an appointment with her pediatrician. The doctor can't find anything wrong, but he books her in for an EEG at the children's hospital in two weeks' time.

In the meantime, India and I visit Margaret and my nephew Rowan at her in-laws' place in Buckhorn, a small town just outside Peterborough, Ontario. One afternoon, we take India swimming at a nearby beach. The water is dark blue and choppy. Margaret and I take turns swimming out to the raft with her. Rowan, who is five, sits on the beach with his grandmother, playing in the sand with his toys. He hates the water. Whenever he calls out to us we call back to him playfully.

As I swim out to the raft with India I notice that her head keeps disappearing under the water. At first I think this is because of the way she's swimming, but I can't spot anything wrong with her technique. She's never been a strong swimmer. Privately Mark and I have always joked she's a sinker like him. Margaret and I grew up swimming at our family's cottage so India's lack of ease in the water worries me.

As India and I tread water by the raft, her head dunks under the water several times. Each time I pull her up. "Are you okay?"

She looks back at me, annoyed. "I'm fine, Mummy. Stop it."

"Are you sure? Are you tired out?"

"I'm okay."

"Maybe you should have a rest."

"Stop it, Mummy. I'm fine. I want to keep swimming."

Margaret joins us at the raft. She watches India's head bob under the water, the way her body seems to empty of energy the way a balloon loses air.

Margaret sees my anxiety and tells me to take a break.

"You have to watch her," I say. "You can't take your eyes off her."

"I will. Don't worry," my sister assures me.

I swim back to the shore, sit at the edge of the beach, watching Margaret and India, ready to dive into the water at any moment.

We visit the second-hand shop in Buckhorn. India and I sort through the toys as Margaret searches for clothes for Rowan. India's wobbly. Her legs quiver and she can't hold herself steady. On our way to the shop she's fallen twice. Her knees are skinned and bloody.

I stay close but when I turn my attention away to look at a book, she collapses and bumps her head. It's the same as the time before – as if she's momentarily abandoned her body.

The episodes are becoming more frequent. One moment India's her usual self, the next she's falling. I'm beginning to worry that Mark is correct and that she's having strokes.

I help her up and sit her in a chair against the wall. I stand at her side afraid to move. India accepts this grudgingly. She wants to keep looking at the toys. A large curvy woman in a white T-shirt and stretch pants walks over to us. She surveys India.

"My daughter used to fall like that," she says flatly.

"She did? What was wrong?"

"Epilepsy. She had epilepsy." I hate her for telling me this. Yet instinctively I understand that the woman's observation might be correct. I quickly picture the only person I'd ever known with epilepsy: Peter, my friend John's flatmate. I stayed with them in Sydenham in South London while I was auditioning for drama school when I was eighteen. Peter was a handsome, regal young man in his twenties who worked at the bank with John. He spoke slowly and with effort. As if every word depleted his resources. He shook continually like an old man with Parkinson's. His fiancée, a small pretty woman who looked as though she belonged to another generation, doted on him. It was difficult for me at that age to separate my opinion of him from the ugliness of the constant jerking. He scared me. In those days, epilepsy was something shameful, as if the sufferer was somehow responsible for the affliction.

I remembered John telling me before I met Peter not to be frightened, describing how he moved and what to do if he had a big attack. I'd been anxious that I'd stare at Peter.

I can't bear the idea of my beautiful child being afflicted with such a frightening disease, a prisoner in constant motion. I stifle an urge to gasp.

"Is your daughter okay?" I ask, starting to cry.

"Oh yes. She's grown up."

"Did the epilepsy go away?"

"No, but –"

"Does she have a job?"

"Of course. She's fine." Then, as if she can sense my fear, she turns on her heels, and leaves the store.

On the way home from the shop, Margaret and I hook our arms through India's. She doesn't like it. But we force her. We practically carry her home.

I've always resented the fact this woman didn't attempt to soften the blow, a reactive response on my part, related I suppose to the old adage "shooting the messenger." Freud considered this kind of reaction a defense mechanism, a way of fighting against the insufferable. Still, I believe were I in this woman's position I would have been kinder, quietly tried to introduce the topic instead of being so blunt.

Many years later, when I ask my sister if she remembers that visit to Buckhorn, she asks, "Do you remember that lady in the shop?"

"Yes, I wish she'd been more gentle," I say softly.

"Yeah, she wasn't mean but she just sort of came out with it. You started crying, remember?"

"No, I'd forgotten."

"I think maybe some part of you already knew."

"Yeah, I was thinking that too." I pause. "It was probably no big deal for that woman. She was used to it. Her daughter was fine. Perhaps she'd forgotten what it was like when she first found out." She wasn't rude, just insensitive, though I'm aware I wasn't ready to hear that anything was wrong with India, particularly this.

Thinking about this time now, I'm ashamed of how much I was in denial. It was just so difficult for me to face the possibility that my daughter might be ill. When I mention this to Margaret, she says, "But why would you want to think that? Nobody wants to admit there's something wrong with their kid. Even India was in denial, don't you remember? We kept telling her she'd fallen and she wouldn't believe us."

I'd forgotten that. It made it harder as India wouldn't listen when we warned her to be careful. She'd repeat over and over, "I didn't fall, Mummy."

The bus back from Buckhorn to Ottawa is dark and half empty. It's late. India sleeps with her head in my lap, her long legs curled towards her chest. As we travel through each small town, the lights flicker over her.

My head buzzes with a constant stream of what-ifs and worry – questions circling around and around, like the darning needle my friends hung over my pregnant belly at my baby shower.

I'm certain now that something is very wrong. When we first got on the bus, I noticed an odd expression in India's eyes, as if they're disappearing along the side of her head. I called her name but she didn't answer me. The attack wasn't long. A second or two at most. When she came to, she caught the expression in my eyes and snapped, "Stop looking at me, Mummy. I'm fine."

Asleep, India occasionally shudders or jerks but for the most part looks peaceful. I can't stop touching her. I stroke her forehead, caress her face, play with her hair.

The bus stops at a gas station and the driver tells us he's taking a fifteen-minute break. Passengers pile out into the night, heading for the store to get snacks and drinks. India stirs, tells me she's thirsty.

"Okay," I say. "But you have to promise me you'll stay in your seat."

"Yes, Mummy. Yes."

"Promise me."

"I will. I will."

"Okay."

I hurry into the shop – grab India a drink and a snack. Stand in the checkout line, impatiently waiting my turn. Every minute seems suspended, slowed down and elongated. My heart wallops in my chest. I want to get back to her.

In the morning at home, Mark and I make India sit on the sofa as we observe her.

We watch episode after episode. It reminds me of a game of peek-a-boo, the kind I played with her when she was a baby. One moment I can see her, the next she disappears. India used to giggle with relief whenever I removed my hands and she could see me. This is how I feel now, every time she returns to her usual self.

We decide to take her to the hospital. When we tell her this she's adamant that she's fine. "We just have to check," we tell her. "Just to be on the safe side."

I don't know how long we wait at the hospital but experience tells me it must have been hours. Finally, we are seen by a young Indo-Canadian doctor with a gentle manner. He watches India, nodding slowly to himself. Then after about half an hour, he books her for an EEG and a CAT scan.

Mark and I disagree over the order of the next two events. Mark says she had the CAT scan and then the EEG. I remember it as the other way around. It's easy to see why we might be confused. Over the course of India's illness there will be so many hospital visits, memories merge into each other. It's like knitting a sweater and trying to remember what you were thinking when you cast on the first row.

This is what I remember.

The EEG room is small and dark. There's a desk with a computer and several large screens. The EEG monitor is threaded with cords as if it's a tree infested with long worms. The technician is in her fifties. Her hair is dyed purplish-red. She has a bunch of teddy bears sitting on her desk.

Mark stands next to India and holds her firmly as she sits on the examining table. He's afraid she will fall forward onto the floor. The technician applies a clear solution on her head, then attaches the electrodes. These are joined to the EEG amplifier, which sends the information to a data acquisition computer. There's a small camera above her. Near that, there's a TV.

"You have so much hair," the technician says. "I'm going to make it messy."

India is transformed slowly. One instant she's herself, the next she's Medusa, her head a mass of snaking cables. She endures the makeover without complaint. The technician, sensing India's nervousness, hands her a teddy bear.

India lies down on the examining table and cuddles it.

The technician seats herself behind the desk. All of a sudden the machines come to life. Lights flicker and flash. The EEG sounds like wind blowing through a tunnel. My daughter is surrounded by equipment I don't understand.

At one point, the technician asks India to breathe slowly. But for the most part, she's free to rest or watch something on TV.

Mark stands near the door, surveying the monitor, slowly trying to decipher the waves on the screen.

"Those are seizures?" he asks, pointing to the lines.

The technician nods.

I look at the screen. Every so often a red line passes over the data. To me, the dark lines look like an angry scrawl.

After about an hour, the test is finished and the technician removes the electrodes. India looks as if she's been through a storm. Her hair is teased high. She starts to hand the teddy bear back to the technician. "It's for you. Keep it," she says kindly.

The technician hands me a printout from the EEG. I study it knowing I won't be able to decipher it. I fold it up and put it in my purse. I store everything connected with India. Sometimes I even keep the tags from new clothing. I stash these things in various boxes around the house. Naturally I don't know that one day I will be thankful for this. Back then, my idea was eventually I would sort these keepsakes out for India and make her a memory book. I got the idea from Mark's dad, who made a volume for each of his four sons. I have nothing from my childhood except photographs. My parents moved too frequently for sentimentality.

Only one parent can accompany India into the CAT scan room. We decide it should be Mark. I wait in the hallway, walk up and down, studying the large black and white Karsh photographs that line the way.

I pray. *Please don't let her die. Don't let it be a tumour. Please let it be epilepsy,* I repeat over and over. I don't know then that people can die from epilepsy.

Eventually Mark and India join me. "That was so cool," India says, running into my arms.

"It was?" I look at Mark.

He shrugs his shoulders. "The machine had a huge *Simpsons* poster on it."

After another long wait we are met by a neurologist called Dr. Humphries. He's an older man, with the air of a history professor. He considers his words cautiously. He's friendly but not effusive.

Here once again, my memory of this differs from Mark's. He says we met with the neurologist outside the EEG room while India slept. But I recall the three of us sitting in Dr. Humphries' office, nervously waiting for the results.

Humphries explains that India has epilepsy. The episodes we'd been witnessing are known as absence seizures. Absence seizures, or *petit mal* – or little bads as I will name them – are caused by abnormal brain functioning. There are two kinds: simple absence seizures and complex absence seizures. The first type, to the casual onlooker, might appear as if the person is simply blanking out or daydreaming. They are brief, lasting only seconds. They can go undetected for years. Complex absence seizures are longer. They can last up to twenty seconds and can be accompanied by lip and hand movements, and blinking. Both can be accompanied by other, more complicated, kinds of seizures. But I don't know that then. I focus on the fact that Dr. Humphries says they are treatable and relatively benign, and that many children grow out of them.

Dr. Humphries gives us a prescription for valproic acid in liquid form. (Later he will prescribe pills as India hates the taste of the liquid.) The syrup has the sticky texture of cough syrup and is the colour of Laura Secord's red lollipops. It smells of artificial cherry. This is the go-to drug for this disorder. It's also prescribed for bipolar disorders and migraines.

At home, when I read the label, I will be alarmed by the long list of side effects: drowsiness, dizziness, headache, diarrhea, constipation, changes in appetite, weight changes, back pain, agitation, mood swings, abnormal thinking, uncontrollable shaking of a part of the body, loss of co-ordination, uncontrollable movements of the eyes, blurred or double vision, ringing in the ears, and hair loss. It can also cause severe liver damage.

I don't recall the neurologist being overly concerned with these, though he does tell us to be on the lookout for a rash, as this indicates a serious intolerance, and to watch her for excessive tiredness. He also tells us she will have to have blood tests to monitor the level of the drug in her bloodstream.

In the years to follow, this list of possible side effects, combined with the long list of side effects from the cock-tail of anti-convulsants she will ultimately be prescribed, will make it difficult for us to gauge the progression of her ill-ness. Mark and I will never be sure which symptoms belong to the disease and which to the supposed treatment. Four years later, when she begins having trouble walking, I will think it's a side effect of one of the drugs. After all, none of her diagnoses mention anything about not being able to walk.

On this day, however, this is not my concern. My child is sick and I want her fixed.

Humphries makes us an appointment for two weeks later so he can monitor the drug's progression. At this time, he explains, we will also meet the nurse in charge of India's case. She will educate us about the intricacies of living with a child with epilepsy, and show us a video about different types of seizures. In the meantime, he seems confident that India can carry on with all her normal activities, with one exception: absolutely no climbing.

Mark and I can't remember how she received this news. She must certainly have been disappointed. She lived to climb. India never did ask a lot about her condition, though once, not long after the initial diagnosis, she asked me if epilepsy would stop her from being a singer.

"No," I said. "It can't do that."

To assure her, I searched the Internet and compiled a list of famous singers and historical figures who had seizures. This pleased her. I feel guilty about this now. I never willingly lied to my child. I had no idea then what we were dealing with.

We leave the hospital and head to our car. Mark pushes India in a wheelchair.

The air is hot and damp after the air-conditioned hospital. It's seven or eight in the evening. The sky is still light but hazy from the heat. As we walk past the Emergency exit, relief floods through me. At the same time there's a sense of grief. A sudden longing for the recent past. I shrug this off. It's temporary, I tell myself. The medicine will make her better.

When I ask Mark how he felt leaving the hospital, he says, "I felt completely shocked. It was the worst thing that ever happened to me. I kept thinking about all the things my asthma had stopped me doing and all the things epilepsy would stop her doing. ... It was the worst thing that had ever happened to me."

We drive to the pharmacy to pick up India's new medication. India sits in the back seat, tilting, head first, to one side whenever she has a seizure, occasionally bumping her head against the window or the car door.

Afterwards, we decide to go to the Dairy Queen in Gatineau, something to cheer us up. Mark knows the route inside out, has driven it countless times. Even so, as we reach the lights at a four-way stop, he drives straight through the red. In over three decades of driving, it's the first time he's ever done this.

3

Motherland

When somebody loved me everything was beautiful.
Every hour we spent together lives within my heart.

And when she was sad I was there to dry her tears.
And when she was happy, so was I.
When she loved me.

– Randy Newman
"When She Loved Me"

I wasn't supposed to be a mother, that's what I'd told myself. I was to get an education and become *something*. My mother frequently told me, if she were to live again, she'd never be a mother. Not that she didn't love my sister and me. It was just she didn't particularly enjoy it. She'd rather be a businesswoman, a chef, or a detective. But secretly even as a teenager I dreamed I'd have a little girl. I'd give her a romantic name, one that sounded as if it belonged to the heroine of a Gothic novel. She'd have a small turned-up nose and black hair. Whenever I pictured us together, I'd see her hand in mine.

Daydreaming about motherhood wasn't what I should've been doing.

My mother's opinions on motherhood must have been deeply ingrained in me. Later, when at thirty I got pregnant, I was so scared of telling her, I got Mark to. She would never get mad at him, I reasoned.

As a teenager, I didn't question my mother's pronouncement. She thought being a mother was an unsuitable pursuit for a woman of intelligence. But nowadays I feel sad on my mother's behalf. I know many of her choices were dictated by the era she grew up in. She most likely yearned for some sort of intellectual satisfaction. She's a smart person with interests in art and literature. I'm sure all the mundane aspects of motherhood bored her.

I can easily imagine what her life might have been like without children. There are so many things she might have done. Usually I picture her as a realtor. My parents have bought and sold more houses than I can remember and it's my mother who's mostly done the prep work. I like to think of my mother pulling up to meet her clients in a red Audi Roadster, wearing a tailored leather jacket over a simple but elegant pantsuit, confident she's made the right choice for her clients.

Still, there's a small part of me that feels hurt and angry about this dismissing of motherhood. I would do anything to be India's mother again.

My mother wanted me to be a lawyer but I knew I was going to be actress. When I was in grade nine, I auditioned for a school production of *The Wizard of Oz*. All the other girls wanted desperately to be Dorothy or Glinda. I wanted to be the Wicked Witch. I admired her fierceness. Unlike the other female characters who might be more sweet-natured, the witch took matters into her own hands. Sure, she was angry, but that made sense to me. After all, Dorothy's house had just landed on her sister. And then there was the matter of those red shoes. Why should she just forgive and forget?

I got the part, but this may very well be because I was the only one who wanted it. The week the show ran I was in heaven. It didn't even matter to me that the cool girls in the cast wouldn't speak to me. When I stood on that stage wearing my drama teacher's black evening gown and the pointy witch's hat that my dad made, I knew I had authority.

I remember the exact moment I felt the audience was under my command. I could feel their eyes on me, waiting to see what I would do next. It was the first time in my life I understood what power was.

Six months after India died, on a day when I was feeling anything but powerful, I visited my favourite second-hand store in the east end of Ottawa. The shop shares its parking lot with a seedy 1960s motel that I suspect rents mostly by the hour. While I was searching the racks a young woman started talking to me. She had dark hair and big blues eyes, and would've been very pretty had she not been covered with scabs. She didn't exactly look like India but her colouring was similar and she reminded me of her. I judged her to be about eighteen. Not much older than India.

She pressed a black halter-top dress against her chest and said to me, "I really like this but I think it's a little sleazy. What do you think?"

I stifled a laugh. Her shorts barely covered her bum. "It's nice. It would look good on you."

She smiled, and continued searching through the dress rack, occasionally asking my opinion on another outfit. I answered her questions, and smiled at her, thinking she sounded lonely and stoned. Eventually I headed towards the book section and we drifted apart. From time to time I would look back and check on her, the way I once had when India and I had gone second-hand shopping together.

We met again at the cash. The older woman standing behind her stood several feet from her as if she was afraid to get too close, sighing impatiently each time the young woman spoke. I wasn't sure what was going on but there seemed to be some sort of problem with what the young woman wanted to buy. This continued for several minutes. Finally, I asked if she needed money.

The young woman smiled. "No, no thank you. I'm okay. It's just they used to let us girls working the street have stuff for free. But the new manager doesn't like it. You know, some of the girls started using in the changing room and just leaving their smelly shoes in the middle of the shop. You know what it's like, it only takes one bad apple."

I smiled as if I understood.

She gathered up her purchases and headed towards the door. "Thank you," she said as she passed me. "That was real nice of you."

The woman in front of me rushed up to the cashier. I leaned against the counter, willing myself not to cry. Over and over I kept thinking, *That's someone's daughter*. I had a daughter. What if this was my girl? Where was her mother? Did she know where her child was? Did she care? Why wasn't she there with her daughter now? I suppose I was making assumptions as well. Wouldn't all mothers do anything for their daughters?

At the same time I was angry with the young woman. Why the hell was she killing herself when she was lucky enough to be alive? For a moment I imagined slamming her against the wall and shouting, "You've got to get it together! You have to save yourself!"

I knew it wasn't right to feel like that. Somewhere along the way she'd been damaged. Nobody would choose to live that way. I suppose she'd decided she was powerless. I understood that. Since India's death, I felt that way as well. But I also remembered what it was to feel strong and command the attention of an audience. Maybe we need those kinds of memories in order to survive the cruel and unexpected.

Mostly I was angry with myself. While we'd been talking I'd wanted say, You need help; it doesn't have to be like this. I'd even thought of inviting her for a coffee. But I hadn't. I was too scared of being ripped off. Not that I really had anything to steal. I only had twenty dollars in cash and my cards could all be cancelled. But perhaps it was more than just fear. Maybe I understood there was nothing I could really do to change her situation. Just like there was no way I could alter my own.

"Life is hard," the cashier answered with a heavy Russian accent.

Mark and I were driving through the outskirts of Chicago on my first Mother's Day without India. I thought I could avoid its trappings by avoiding Facebook. The year before, India barely woke up on Mother's Day, and reading about all the fun things people were doing with their mothers had driven me to tears.

Everywhere there were gas stations, flower shops, and restaurants proclaiming Happy Mother's Day. I tried listening to the radio, hoping to distract myself, but even that proved painful. The smooth-voiced DJ talked about his mother, listeners phoned in requesting songs for their mothers, and restaurants advertised their special Mother's Day brunch.

Suddenly, I spotted a chain restaurant a friend had recommended. Food – the perfect distraction. We headed off the highway, into a suburb I could've called Anywhere North America. We followed the signs, farther and farther from the highway. Finally, we found it. My stomach grumbled with hunger, but we never even made it into the parking lot. From the road we could see the lineup was so long customers were standing on the porch.

Unlike the young woman in the thrift store, my marginalization isn't visible, though in my mind I look like one of those transparent anatomical manikins at the science museum. I'm always shocked when people tell me I look good. Someone peering into our car that Mother's Day would never have known by looking at me the significance of that day. The circles around my eyes might be the result of one too many late nights or a stressful job. They'd never have guessed it was my first as a bereaved mother.

It bothers me that we don't take the time to look at people closely enough to see that they might be struggling. The car travelling ahead on the road – perhaps that driver is going slowly for a reason. Maybe his mother just died, or she's on the way to a bereavement group, or he simply can't stop crying.

The truth is a society that has embraced a death-denying culture renders many in mourning powerless, but it is particularly disempowering to those of us who have lost loved ones unexpectedly and out of sequence – especially when it's children. We are invisible. Strangers at the mall tut at me impatiently as I meander slowly in front of them. Cashiers roll their eyes when I fumble through my bag looking for my debit card. I've cried in so many public places now I don't even consider how it must look.

In a chain restaurant in Missoula, Montana – ironically the one I was so anxious to try out on that first Mother's Day – I started to cry when I realized I couldn't eat my dinner. Finally, I had my plate of collard greens and candied sweet potatoes and my stomach was as tightly sprung as an India rubber ball. The waitress, a young plump woman with masses of blonde hair, noticed and asked me if I was okay. Mark said he was sure she thought he'd done something. I mumbled something about suffering a loss. It was near closing time. She told me sweetly to stay as long as I needed.

These days, I have a lot in common with the guy begging in front of the liquor store. Some may choose to acknowledge me, but most don't. I've begun to notice that some people look away when I mention my daughter's name in the same way my dog looks away when he knows he's in trouble.

Not only have I lost my place in society, but I've lost my identity, which, despite being a feminist, was largely founded on the fact that I was India's mother. Who am I without her? It's like waking up one morning to discover that you're unable to do what you are best at. I'm the pianist whose fingers are broken. I was my very best when I mothered my daughter. At the same time, I'm not as free as that pianist. I must think before I share my experience. My loss makes everyone uncomfortable. But to keep silent demands I lie about my life or pretend. It's no small thing.

If I were younger, thirty or thirty-five, it might be easier to envisage a future. There would be the luxury of time. Given the opportunity, I might have even considered being a mother once again.

This is not an option now; many of my peers are becoming grandparents. I never knew I wanted to be a grandmother until my daughter died. Disaster has a great deal to do with timing.

In my early fifties, I'm aware that more of the sand in my hourglass is at the bottom. I'm at a point in life where I should know my place in the world, but I'm as shaky as the shy grade nine girl who has decided to ask the boy she likes out on a date. The thumping in my heart tells me it could go either way.

Grief has the power to bring back all one's old failures and losses. In the midst of mourning my child, I find myself back in the past, questioning old decisions, reliving make-or-break moments. Emotional wounds I'd long ago buried.

When India was alive I never cared that I didn't have an important career or made a lot of money – I was happiest mothering my daughter and living a creative life. Now I feel I have lost everything. I wonder if my life has been wasted. Should-I-haves and what-ifs dot the landscape of my regrets. I'm trying to figure out how I can regain power over my life again, but the answer eludes me.

"Why did you only have one?" a well-meaning friend asked one night after several beers. Then, realizing how the question sounded, she apologized immediately.

"It's okay," I said. "It's a fair question. The truth is I only ever wanted one child. I thought that way I could give them all the great things I had as a kid. I knew I'd never have money."

Looking back, do I wish I'd had more children? No. I only want my daughter back.

Everything is different now. People who used to call, don't, and I no longer feel comfortable in many social situations I used to enjoy. As an extrovert I was the queen of small talk. Now I find it exhausting and gravitate towards conversations that matter and people who have also known loss or are unafraid to confront it, people willing to understand how it feels to grieve.

"Putting yourself in someone else shoes is a very radical act," my friend Janet, a United Church minister, told me after India died. "It can mean questioning your own values or your preconceived notions about someone. That's why so few are willing to go there."

A month after India died, my friend Una took me out to our village pub. I was having a rough day. I kept bursting out into sobs. I was still trying to accept that India had died, which sounds strange as I'd seen her die, but it was almost as if my body couldn't absorb it. I didn't know what to do with myself. The only thing that gave me comfort was sitting on the front porch smoking one cigarette after another. I hadn't smoked since India was born, but as soon as I heard she was dying, I took it up again with a vengeance.

I'd smoke and look into the autumn sun and talk to her. "Mummy loves you," I'd say or "Why won't you come back?" or "Please, please, baby, come back." Sometimes I thought I heard her calling me: "Mummy, Mummy, Mummy."

I was grateful to Una for getting me out of the house. We took a corner seat and ordered beer. We'd only been sitting there a few minutes when a woman I knew casually from the village noticed me. At the sight of me, her jaw dropped as if she'd just witnessed a car accident – only I was the accident. Immediately I backed as far as I could into my seat. It was no good. She leaned towards me and said, "I'm so sorry, I just don't know what to say to you. I just don't know what to say to you. I just don't know –"

"It's okay," I said.

I saw a flash of concern in Una's eyes.

"My God, I just don't know what to say to you. I'm so sorry –"

"It's okay," Una said. "She knows you're sorry."

That night sticks with me. I never expected shame to be a feeling I connected with loss, but I felt as if I'd been caught stealing or making love to my best friend's husband. I suppose I feel shameful because I don't like people to feel sorry for me. There is of course a legitimate reason for their pity but it makes me feel weak. Or maybe it's just my British heritage. I was always taught to hold back my feelings and not show my emotions. I was never very good at this but it's ingrained in my psyche. I know people whisper about me. I accept that. I understand I'm living proof that bad things happen to nice people. *If it could happen to my family, it could happen to yours.* There's shame attached to that. Surrounded by a group of mothers talking about their children, I shrink, will myself to disappear. Naturally I have opinions about what they are discussing, but I'm afraid to say anything. Even though logically I know I did everything I could for my child, I'm very much aware I failed. Why would anyone want to hear from me? I'm the mother of the dead girl.

People worry so much about saying the wrong thing. They don't want to accidentally say something that upsets me. I appreciate this. They're also afraid of how they will feel if this happens. I – not just me but the bereaved in general – make them afraid, vulnerable, but worst of all, ashamed. But what is it that makes them feel this way? Is it because I make them aware of how little they appreciate their good fortune? Or that we are all so defenceless? We like to think we have control over our world, but a grieving parent is proof that's an illusion.

Most of the time it's not what people say that hurts. It's driving home at night past my neighbour's house, and catching sight of a lit TV screen and imagining they're getting ready to watch a Friday night movie as I used to do with my daughter. It's just being here, existing in the world. The way I feel compelled to say, "I'm okay" whenever I'm asked, "How are you doing?" Though I rarely am. I do this not because I'm unwilling to share my real sentiments – I simply know most people don't really want to know. Grief is like walking across hot coals with a smile on your face. Behind every corner or across every street lies the possibility of accidental pain. The happy ending of that action-packed movie where the child runs into his mother's arms calling her name makes most viewers smile with relief, but for me it is just more evidence of what I've lost.

I was surprised when I first became a mother how it broadened my consciousness. I suddenly understood that everyone was someone's child, and because of that, I could connect with, and open up to, people I never would have in the past. I felt their concerns and marvelled at how my universe expanded. Confronted by the young woman in the thrift store, my mind immediately connected to her mother.

In September 2014, while we were still living in Wakefield, Quebec, an eleven-year-old girl was struck by a falling tree during a severe storm and died. She was out playing in a forest, near her backyard, probably with her brothers and sisters. The photos in the local newspaper showed a girl with a relaxed smile and brilliant eyes, her black hair tied in a long ponytail. I expect that once the young woman in the thrift store looked very similar.

I was at our local pub when I heard the news. The woman who told me was visibly upset, but I knew she didn't really know what it meant. Before my daughter's death I would probably not have lingered on the story, but for days afterwards I couldn't stop thinking about the girl's mother. I'd imagined her at home on a pleasant Sunday afternoon, perhaps getting the evening meal ready. Not a clue that in minutes her life would be irrevocably damaged. Maybe she took a moment to ponder her good fortune. Most likely she was just happy that all her children were outside and she was enjoying being by herself.

When I envision this mother now, she's engulfed in fog. Wakefield lies on the Gatineau River and some days the fog is so heavy it covers the highway. It can look like a scene from a 1940s British mystery. Drivers can see only a few feet in front of them. In my mind's eye, I see this mother in the thick of it.

I imagine her searching throughout the days for clues that her daughter still exists in the universe. Watching for birds, the way the sun streams through the trees, traces of her being, something to grasp. Mothers don't leave their children behind.

On the day of the girl's funeral, a group of friends hung purple balloons through the village in her honour. They were everywhere: in front of the bakery, the pet shop, the school, the local pub. Purple must have been the girl's favourite colour. I watched them toss in the September breeze, thought of India. She also liked purple. How many girls love purple? How many girls won't get to grow up?

I wanted to connect with the girl's mother even though we'd never met. To give her comfort, even though I knew there was nothing I could say. Instead I bought her groceries: cheese, hummus, apples, cookies, juice. I thought at least I could give her a break from some of her duties.

I left a note telling her that I was India's mother – I knew she'd know who India was. Everyone in the village did – and I was thinking of her and that if she ever needed to talk to contact me. She never did. I knew she probably wouldn't, but I'd hoped to tell her in person that I understood.

Strange to discover that grief, like motherhood, widens our ability to feel for others.

Yet I've changed. I don't have the patience I once had and find myself blurting out feelings that I once would have censored. At first I tried to stop it, push it down. I was afraid I was becoming mean, but I merely don't have the energy for superficiality. Grief seems to amplify everyday cruelties the same way taking a finicky friend camping suddenly makes all their fussy quirks seem annoying.

It's as if I'm an apple and I've been peeled all the way down to my core, to the teenager I was when I played the Wicked Witch of the West, that girl who was terrified of forgetting her lines but stepped out on the stage anyway. Once there, I instantly forgot my fear, I was so immersed in my role. Nowadays this fear is replaced with a new one. Do I dare reveal my vulnerability?

The only time I ever questioned my choice to play the witch was after a matinee performance at a local grade school when the kids gathered about the other leads, but avoided me. I even remember telling them, "I'm not really a witch. It's just a costume," but none of them would chance it.

Now every time I leave my house and meet someone new I face a similar dilemma. Do I reveal the actor under the costume or do I just pretend to be that confident middle-aged woman who's learned how to make everyone else comfortable?

Grief is teaching me a great deal about risks: those I'm willing to take and those who are willing to take them with me. Like the Wicked Witch, I may live on the outskirts, and may even be feared by society, but there's opportunity in that. A chance to finally get those ruby red shoes – or at least be free to wear the shoes that really fit. Not long after India died, I told my friend Andrea that as a bereaved mother I no longer fit in. Andrea, an artist and a young widow, answered, "Did you ever?"

In an odd way it makes sense that I have more in common with my teenage self than the middle-aged woman I've become. In the last two years of India's life, I spent more time talking to her than some people ever spend with their children. I mothered her but I was also cast in the role of teenage companion.

I watched hours of *Buffy the Vampire Slayer* and swooned with her over the good but troubled vampire, Angel, and the bad vampire, Spike. We danced together to Eminem. As the disease progressed, tucked in her bed, she moved her trembling arms as best she could, while I pranced around her room, the music so loud we had to shout at each other.

We even talked about the two boys she loved: one sweet-natured but brooding, the other confident and chatty. I liked the chatty one who visited, and at school spun her around in the wheelchair. She kept his scarf tied around the headboard of her bed. But when I said one time, "You should go out with him," she retorted, "You go out with him if you like him so much."

A couple of weeks after India died, I was driving downtown and saw a billboard for the Scotiabank which featured the image of a mother holding her new baby in a pink blanket. The caption read, *The moment everything changes.* Instantly I was drawn back into the room at Roger's House, the children's hospice, where I watched my child die.

Ever since that moment I've had to accept that my

future is no longer tied to India's. Not that I ever believed for an instant she'd feel compelled to look after me or live close by when she grew up – I understood she had dreams in which I didn't play a role. Instead I envisioned myself fixed to her as if she were a brightly coloured kite and I the ribbon tied to her tail.

These days when I look at myself in the mirror, the face I see is entirely different from the one I remember. It's like looking into the eyes of a junkyard dog that's been beaten. I can tell by the creases around her eyes she's seen more than she wants to remember and that if I push too hard she just might bite.

Four months after India died, Mark and I stopped at the local hippy place for dinner. It was late so I thought it would be relatively child free. But next to every empty table there was either a group of glowing pregnant women or a newborn nestled against its mother. Finally, we opted for the table next to a family with two young boys. However, as soon as I began to eat, I noticed a mum rocking a newborn baby and I was besieged with memories: the softness of my daughter's skin, the weight of her in my arms, the way she smelled of talcum powder and yeast.

Onlookers probably thought I was crying because Mark and I were having an argument. Bereaved parents don't exist in the public's consciousness and with the exception of the news or the movies we don't get much media attention. If you're trying to sell laundry detergent, we're probably not your best bet. These days being in the world feels like showing up in a tennis outfit when everyone is out on the ice playing hockey.

Twenty years ago, when I took Women Studies at Carleton University, our professor asked us to decide which we considered more fundamental to our sense of identity: our race or gender. Like the majority of white women, I chose my gender, whereas the women from minority groups all tended to choose race. I was surprised by this, but the professor explained that often the part of ourselves we most strongly identify with is the part that has been most threatened. Lately I've been thinking about that as I grapple with the fact I now identify as a bereaved mother, who is, for the most part, invisible.

Like Lord Voldemort in J.K. Rowling's Harry Potter series, death is attached to my name. I'm the you-know-who something terrible happened to. It's dangerous to speak my name. Better to pretend that mothers like me don't exist. Hide us under the bed with all the things that go bump in the night and those who must not be named.

Funnily enough, in an interview in 2005 with Melissa Anelli and Emerson Spartz of TheLeakyCauldron.org ("The Leaky Cauldron and Mugglenet Interview, Part Three," July 16, 2005), Rowling said, "Voldemort's fear is death, ignominious death. I mean, he regards death itself as ignominious. He thinks that it's a shameful human weakness, as you know." She cleverly created a villain that taps into our communal shame. This also explains my shame. I was unable to save my daughter from a slow, painful death, and the gradual loss of her gifts and skills. Even though there was nothing I could do, I live with the fact that I failed her. This isn't rational, but I'm ashamed I survived her.

Most of my friends are careful about talking to me about their kids, but in my grief group this was not case. I used to hate going because of this. Throughout the meeting, I'd fight the urge to grab my coat and run. The problem was I was overwhelmed with a sense of envy, jealous of the bereaved parents in the group with other children. This guilt combined with my sadness was stifling. I knew their grief was as painful as mine and that it was wrong to compare my situation with theirs. So my feelings troubled me. It was their status as parents, not their pain, that I envied. They were still families. Mothers and fathers.

I liked being a mother; I was good at it – and before you think it, I'll just say it: yes, I'll always be India's mother, but I'm no longer engaged in the act of mothering her. This is a huge distinction. I miss mothering my daughter. I miss buying her funky socks at Target, cooking her dinner, kissing her goodnight, fighting with her. Things we don't usually think about. India and I will not make new memories together. I will have to survive on what I have. When I post a photo of her on Facebook, I'm aware that eventually I will run out of photos one day. I have to be content with the reminders I have. From now on, our relationship will be built on my imaginings. What might she have become? Who would she have loved? Where would she have lived?

The night I revealed my secret to the group, we had guest speakers, parents who were alumni of our group. They shared the story of their child's death and how their lives had evolved in the following five years. The couple, though clearly heartbroken, had gone on to adopt children. The story was beautiful but it saddened me. How did parents without children continue on? When I questioned the group about this, everyone misunderstood and began telling me I could adopt. Perhaps if I was younger, but now, after spending six years struggling with the medical community and India's illness, it's impossible.

On my way home from the meeting, I was reminded of a conversation I had with one of India's nurses shortly after she died. We were standing by the window, and the sun was pouring in. Everything that day seemed more intense. It was like looking at the world through a kaleidoscope. The light in the trees shimmered, and the air around me seemed to crackle as if it had been infused with electricity. I told the nurse I didn't know how I would survive. She said India would tell me, that parents often told her their children led them to what they were supposed to do.

My grief counsellor frequently uses the term *transformative* when she talks about grief. When she originally used this term I balked. I thought it was in line with all the usual worn-out platitudes, like Be positive; Time heals all wounds; At least she's no longer in pain; or, my personal favourite, The Lord – sometimes this is changed to The world – never gives us more than we can handle.

Lately I've begun to revisit this word. Now I'm reminded of the tarot card, The Tower. Though there are many visual interpretations of The Tower, the one I'm familiar with is the image of a tall burning tower being struck by lightning. This is why it's associated with impending doom or disaster. I like the following reading: Downfall – Ruin – Ego blow – Explosive transformation. The type of transformation that is thrust upon a person.

I think of myself as a city that has been bombed and is forced to rebuild. I don't know why disaster strikes some people while others go unscathed. That night after the meeting I came to the conclusion India wouldn't like it if I became a mum again. She used to tell me off if I showed any of my students too much affection. She never liked to share.

All I ever wanted for India was for her to be healthy and able to pursue what gave her joy. I know she wants the same for me. One of the grief platitudes I've grown to despise is, "She's not really gone. She lives on inside you." During the early stages of grief, I was still polite and I would nod and say, "Thank you." When I really just wanted to say *Fuck you, I don't want her there, I want to have her here, where I can talk to her.*

Now that my teenage self – that girl who played the Wicked Witch – is rearing her head, I might say that. But what if there's a smidgen of truth in what they said? What if I'm adopting some of her traits? Maybe her gift to me is that I'm becoming more like her. I don't mean in that she lives in my heart – yes, of course, she does, forever – but in her resistance to allowing her disease to define her, she's taught me to do the same with my status. Maybe, just maybe, that resilience was something she inherited from me that I'd forgotten about until now. She hated it when people tried to pigeonhole her as the sick girl. She knew she was more than that. If I follow her example, maybe people will be forced to see the entire me, not just the bereaved mother.

When I doubt myself, I should think of India at her last school dance. Mark and I were parked outside the school. The teachers were worried about the dance bringing on a big seizure, so we agreed to stay close. We didn't want to crowd her, so we sat in the car watching Netflix.

It was Hallowe'en. The dance was in the school's basement. There was no wheelchair access so with the help of some of her pals we carried her down to it in her wheelchair. Mark had painted India's face white and covered it with thin blue lines so that she looked like Willow, the witch from the TV show *Buffy the Vampire Slayer* in the episode where she is transformed from good Willow to evil Willow after her girlfriend is murdered. Her lipstick was a blackish-blue, which made the inside of her mouth look a deep red. She made a very menacing witch, in her black leather jacket and black leggings, sneering at us and pretending to cast spells.

As we sat in the car, we could see the lights flickering from the dance. Even as close as we were it was difficult not to worry. We never knew what to expect. Everyday events for others often morphed into the horrific for us. At one point, I couldn't resist taking a peek through the window. AC/DC's "Hell's Bells" was blasting from the speakers. India was on the dance floor, three girls dancing around her wheelchair as she waved her arms to the beat.

I like to think India was just another teenage girl at a dance that night, her friends just happy to be having fun with her. And though she couldn't move as freely as them in some ways, perhaps in a spiritual sense, she was freer, for she knew what it was like to want to dance and to do it despite the constraints. I have to remember that. Especially on the mornings when it would be easiest to pull the covers over my head and give in to grief.

The summer India turned fifteen she was in the hospital forty-seven days. Her neurologist ordered a particularly nasty test to rule out a disease he was concerned about: Batten disease. The test consisted of taking some of her skin because they were going to grow her cells in their lab. They were looking for "foamy cells," misshapen cells that looked like "half moons and fingerprints," according to The National Institute of Neurological Disorders and Stroke. Like all the other diseases she was tested for, this one was deadly. Mark and I tried our best to explain what was going to happen. India was nervous but willing. She'd recently lost the use of her legs and she wanted to know why.

India and I sat in her room waiting for the test most of the day, me sipping cold coffee and trying to get comfortable in the blue vinyl visitor's chair, which doubled as my bed. India was in her "I heart boys with British accents" T-shirt and her purple glasses, watching hours of anime and giggling wildly whenever a character fell in love or lost their temper.

The doctor who showed up to administer the test was a handsome Indo-Canadian man in his early thirties. With his high-top running shoes and striped polo shirt, he looked like he belonged in a recording studio rather than a lab. He sat down next to India and said, "This isn't going to hurt. I do this to myself all the time."

He did the test quickly. India winced; her green eyes grew large and wet. The two bleeding puncture marks in her skin looked like vampire bites.

"You must be crazy if you do that to yourself," she said. "That hurt *a lot.*"

My mother would have gotten mad at me for saying that. She would have said I was being cheeky. She would've thought I was embarrassing her. I was proud of India. She'd told the truth.

I'm not sure what he said next, but it was probably something like, "I'm not crazy – you are. That didn't hurt."

She looked at him, raising her eyebrow, amused perhaps. She was used to entertaining doctors.

"A while back, we had another kid that nobody could diagnose. But now we know," he said, shaking the little vial of India's skin.

I smiled. There was nothing to say. I couldn't figure out what would be worse, not knowing or knowing. Both frightened the hell out of me.

India once said to me, "Mummy, doctors mustn't have any feelings. They always say things aren't going to hurt but they always do."

They always hurt her. Watching your child endure pain is something no parent should experience. I spent six years doing this. Sometimes while a nurse was putting in the IV, I'd get so angry that I imagined pulling her off my daughter and viciously inserting the needle into her vein.

Other times, I'd take out my knitting and focus on it. People probably thought I was so used to the procedure that I didn't care. Though India rarely cried, I could see on her face how much it hurt. She had tiny veins. Baby veins, one nurse called them.

After living this kind of life it's hard to understand why anyone would care about their kid's math mark.

The last time India was in the hospital before she died, they were trying an experimental steroid treatment that might have prolonged her life. When I slept next to her on the little cot, we held hands all night long. We'd done this before. But there was a difference in her grip – as if she was grasping onto me, afraid I'd let go. If I had to go to the bathroom, I'd hold it in, waiting for her to fall asleep, then sneak away when I was desperate, afraid she'd know I'd gone.

Before this, when she was in the hospital she watched movies for hours. But this time the computer screen blurred for her and the images jumped. This was the beginning of the end. And I couldn't face it. Who could?

Yes, they'd told me she was going to die, but to accept that kind of fact is to go against all the principles of motherhood. From the time my girl was born, I knew I would do anything for her. So how could I accept the possibility of her dying?

Death was coming. India's face was changing. Her pale creamy skin was a sickly yellow, a colour I'd seen only on my friend Diana when she was dying. I tried to prepare myself. I read books about grief and death, blogs by bereaved parents. Terrifying.

On our third day in the hospital, I was lying on the bed chatting with India, probably trying to make her laugh. It was my favourite thing to do. She liked to tease me back too. Shauna, her caregiver, was lying at the end of the bed. We were a tag team, both working to distract her, keep the hallucinations away.

A doctor and a nurse from Roger's House, the children's hospice, tapped on the door. They leaned into the room and introduced themselves. They wore dark colours; their shoulders were rounded and tensed. To me, they looked like two black crows, circling the graveyard in a horror movie.

I shouted at them, my voice high-pitched and shrill. In my mind they were harbingers of death. If they entered her room, she would die.

They apologized quietly and closed the door discreetly.

I met the nurse, Marion, several months later. She ran the small bereavement group Mark and I were members of.

"I was rude to you. Shouted for you to get out," I said after group one night.

She nodded.

"I'm sorry," I said. "I didn't want her scared."

"You don't have to apologize ever," she said. "You were looking after your girl."

Yes, I thought I was doing my job. I was being India's mother.

I met Marion again recently as I was on the way to visit my grief counsellor who works at the hospice. I told her I was writing about that time. She said, "I have a theory. When a parent's child is sick, they go crazy. But when their child is dying, they're psychotic."

I asked her if I could quote her and she told me to go right ahead.

Nine months after India's death, I had a studio in an old school in the village of Farrellton, just north of Gatineau Park. I shared it with Una, who is also a writer. The rest of the twenty residents were visual artists. The window in our room overlooked an old playground filled with metal frames of swing sets and monkey bars, the kind of play structure long ago banished from the parks India visited.

Una and I shared a long desk and bulletin board. On her side of the board there was a painting she did of a man's chest; a poem she wrote that was published in *Arc Magazine*; a printout of a photograph of her family taken in the '70s; a long collage featuring a sink, a typewriter, and a man hanging on to a speeding boat for dear life; and a sign that said, "Sorry, we're sorry."

My things dominated the space: a postcard of a sculpture by Anslem Kiefer; *Book With Wings 1992*, an unfinished fibre piece I had started months before, constructed from a little girl's red cardigan with two singing birds on it, the word "grieve" embroidered in pink; a doll I made of a naked man and a red guitar; a birthday card India had given me with the Eiffel Tower on it; my front of house photograph from when I used to act; an embroidered piece I made that reads "A short history of you"; and a photocopy of a painting my friend Erin did of India as Persephone – Did she see what was coming or was it just a coincidence?

In the winter I used to go there to write but would end up crying instead. I missed India so much all I wanted to do was look at photographs of her or listen to her music: the soundtracks from *Wicked*, *Rent*, and *Sweeney Todd*; albums by Bedouin Soundclash, Luke Doucet, Johnny Cash, Fiona Apple, and Lily Allen. Some of these I can listen to now. Others I can't.

I kept a lot of my India treasures there: a photograph of her at her art class with bleached blonde hair, her cat Stuffie, a small piece of paper on which she wrote the word paper – I have no idea why but it doesn't matter; this paper is invaluable to me.

When I couldn't write I sewed. I'm usually an avid knitter but I had no desire to do it. Maybe it wasn't engaging enough. I needed something that required my complete attention. So I began making sewn posters; I'd done this before when India was in the hospital. One day it struck me how nobody at the hospital ever asked me how I was. I might be walking down the hall crying and the hospital staff would look away. I decided if I felt like this, other parents must as well. So I embroidered a big sign that said, "It's going to be okay." I hung it on a tree in front of the hospital which some kids had decorated with beads. It's a place where I used to take India to sit in the sun.

I continued making the signs even through the last weeks of her life. I hung them at the heart institute, the General Hospital, the park I took India to as a child. They said things like Breathe, Forgive, Don't give up. Were these words just platitudes? Or prayers?

Prayers, I think. Reminders to myself to forge on. Believe that there was still the possibility things could get better.

A couple of weeks before India died I made a large quilted piece that said, "The hardest thing about life is learning when to hang on and when to let go." Looking back, I understand that the act of sewing this was my way of working on acceptance, admitting I had no control over the future. I hung it in Wakefield in the park facing the river. After she died I noticed someone placed a bouquet of flowers under it.

Mark and I took several long trips after India died. We went to Mexico, drove west across the States, ending up in Vancouver, and then flew to Japan. Each time I was away from home I felt more and more free. I still grieved; there's no way to run from loss, or at least not any I've discovered. But on the road, if someone asked me if I had children, I could choose to lie or simply answer yes. It gave me a sense of control over my life.

In Wakefield I couldn't do that. I had to tell three people in one day India died. Then, as if that wasn't enough, I ended up comforting them. As if it were my fault. That wasn't supposed to be my role, but I couldn't just stand there and watch people cry.

Initially, each time I told someone it was like having to say it for the very first time. This I remember well. My friend Anita took us for brunch at a café that had held a benefit for India. I was just about to sit down when an older woman touched my shoulder.

"Hi Lesley, I was at India's benefit. How's she doing?" she asked. "I keep her in my prayers."

"She passed," I said, unable to say the word died. The café was quiet and I felt like everyone was looking at me. Strangely, it felt as if I was on stage – but as a powerless character, one who is killed off in the first act.

I remember feeling badly for the woman. I knew she would be sad and sorry that she'd asked. She was being kind. I didn't hold it against her.

"I'm so sorry," she said.

"Thank you," I replied, taking my seat.

Mark and I decided, when we headed west through the States to Vancouver, a stopover on our way to Japan, that if we wanted something, we'd treat ourselves. By the time we returned to Quebec in the middle of June, the backseat of our car was heaving with souvenirs: a key chain from the Rock and Roll Hall of Fame and Museum in Cleveland, Ohio; a pair of bullet earrings from Mount Baker City in Oregon; funky blue socks from Hood River, also in Oregon; red and teal cowboy boots from Cody, Wyoming; a hand-dyed pink silk shawl bought in Kyoto, Japan; red long johns from Yellowstone National Park; two yellow vintage Pyrex dessert cups found second-hand somewhere in Minnesota. With each purchase, there'd be a rush of happiness; a friend of mine who lost her husband told me that the first year after his death she bought shoes constantly. The excitement of the purchase never lasted. I'd remember that India would never see it and then I'd get sad.

In Gibsons, British Columbia, I bought myself a dress on a whim. The dress had a halter top and a wide 1950s skirt. It was sky blue and covered with pirate flags. I knew India would approve, though she probably would have told me it was too low cut. She would've have called it "slitty," our word for slutty. We'd started using it when she was about twelve. She'd overheard some girls call another a slut but misheard them and thought they'd said slit. So after a con-versation about the origins of slut shaming, we'd adopted the word slitty for clothes that were risqué.

I never censored India's taste. A romantic with a flair for the dramatic, she favoured Manga-inspired outfits over low-cut T-shirts and short skirts. She often looked as if she'd stepped out of an anime movie.

We still have her clothes. Everything is packed in big blue Tupperware boxes. Among them, a cream-coloured satin Regent style wedding dress she liked because it looked like it belonged to a Jane Austen character, and a Goth evening gown which, when she was sick, she used to watch TV in. I have no idea what will become of these things.

Whenever I buy clothes, the first thing I ask myself is if India would approve. She was very opinionated about how I should dress. Once when I was wearing white pants, she told me, "Mummy, you can't wear white. You're not Beyoncé."

I don't know what I said but I'm pretty sure I laughed. Now I don't ever wear white. Too afraid. India might strike me down with a lightning bolt.

The halter-top dress from Gibsons needed to have the straps adjusted. The vendor, who was also the dressmaker, said it would only take her a few minutes to fix them. I could tell in the way she came behind me and played with the straps and joked about my ample bosom that if I lived in Gibsons we could be friends. I judged her to be in her mid-fifties. In her presence I felt like just another lady buying a pretty dress.

As she started to sew, her phone rang. She excused herself and answered it. "Oh no," I heard her say. "I'm so sorry, sweetheart. Don't worry. I can lend you my car."

From her tone I could tell she was talking to her child. I didn't know what to do with myself. I stood there, arms dangling, quietly wondering if this was how life would be from now on: those who had families ... and me, forever existing on the periphery. Like the Lady of Shalott, continually forced to look at the present through the distortion of the past, my daughter's image forever reflected in the eyes of those who love their children.

She hung up. "My daughter's car keeps breaking down. She's sunk all her money into it."

India couldn't wait to learn to drive. She used to tell me she'd never take another bus when she grew up. She thought it was crazy that I didn't learn to drive until I was forty-two. My fear of all things mechanical was beyond her comprehension. When I'd fumble with the TV remote control, she'd snatch it from my hands. "You do it like this," she'd say.

"Do you have any kids?" the dressmaker asked.

"No," I said after a long pause, hating myself for lying. I didn't want to tell this woman the truth. She'd be kind. Ask thoughtful questions. Tell me she *couldn't imagine* what I'd been through.

I knew she could. Any mother who has sat with her child while they've battled a fever has an idea of what I've been through. It's just nobody wants to visit the place where I live. I don't blame them. It's like that scary old house in *Psycho* where Norman Bates lives with his dead mother. Every room is etched with the possibility of danger: the corpse of a loved one, the torment of mistakes and memories. There's nowhere to hide. Better to pretend that children don't die. Safer not to think about that scary old house and focus on the pretty houses on your street. I wish to God I didn't know.

This was the first time I'd ever denied India's existence. I didn't want to. I just couldn't stand to feel the weight of this woman's pity. My bereavement is not how I want to be remembered. I'm more than my loss.

I made a silent apology to India. She'd understand. She'd always hated it when people saw her as just the girl in the wheelchair.

I didn't become a mother until I was thirty-one. When I was pregnant I used to play music to my belly. I was teaching drama in those days and one of my students, who was an accomplished musician, told me his mother had read a study saying playing Mozart to babies improved their intellects. I didn't mind Mozart but I wanted my child to be a free thinker, so I leaned my swollen belly against the big speaker in our living room and played John Lennon. Apart from taking prenatal vitamins and all the usual precautions, including quitting smoking, this was the only way I prepared for motherhood.

Later, when India was born, I made my one and only conscious choice about mothering. I decided I didn't want to be the kind of mother who expected her child to make her proud. Growing up, I hated it when my mother would say, even jokingly, "Go and make me proud." It felt as if I'd been brought into the world to live out her dreams instead of my own. It made me feel like a possession. As if my accomplishments weren't the result of hard work but instead bestowed on me through ancestry. I didn't want that for my daughter. It was essential to me that India feel like a person in her own right. Our children are not our possessions.

Instead of kids making their parents proud, I thought it should be the other way around. So I decided I would endeavour to do just that. I understood the only way for me to accomplish this was to fulfill my own promise (something that sounds simple now but at the time was daunting). It meant becoming a writer. Later on, whenever I contemplated quitting writing, I'd think about India and how if I didn't stick to my dream she'd never learn how to fight for her own.

At times this was difficult, particularly when she was a baby and I'd force myself to write while she napped. There were days when I wanted nothing more than to sleep with her.

When she first died I couldn't look at little girls, especially babies and toddlers. People were surprised by this. They thought it would be teenagers.

The truth is I never got to experience mothering a teenager in all its complexity. Yes, my daughter frequently shouted at me. Yes, she told me she hated me. But we rarely got to do the normal things. A trip to the mall with a fifteen-year-old girl in a wheelchair who seizes constantly is a major undertaking. Plus she was so tired. Often just the drive to the mall wore her out.

When she was little my biggest concern was her constant climbing. She was always hanging off things: the sink, a tree, the monkey bars. If it was climbable she'd be there.

In the early days of grief, any time a mother would bring her new baby or two-year-old into the shop where I worked I'd feel the corner of my mouth begin to tremble. I'd repeat over and over in my head that *it's going to be okay*.

This is a part of grief I didn't know about. I'd never experienced this kind of envy before. Sure, I'd envied people their successes but never their whole lives. Recently I've been reading about the Salem witch trials. One of the accused, a prosperous farmer named Giles Corey, refused to enter a plea of guilty or not guilty so he had thirty-two boulders pressed on his stomach. This is how it felt when I saw mothers with their little girls – as if they were all standing on top of my chest. Like that illustration from the Musicians of Bremen, where the animals are all on top of each other.

The mothers would wander around the shop, babies in arms or toddlers by the hand, and I would force myself to watch, will my voice to be steady, my hands not to shake. They had no idea what their presence evoked in me. How could they? How could we exist if we knew the pain our happiness caused others?

One day after a gruelling session with my grief counsellor, I decided to go to the nail spa I used to visit with India. It seemed like a way to treat myself. As soon as I entered the spa I was comforted by the familiar smell of lemon and camphor. On the front desk there was a vase filled with a fabric rose and a bowl of tiny papaya candies, the kind India loved. The walls were covered with posters of beautiful Asian women with childish smiles and nails that looked like brightly coloured plastic knives. The woman at the desk motioned me to a massage chair in the middle of the row and I obeyed. On the TV, one of India's favourite movies, *She's the Man*, was playing. I'd seen it at least ten times. I watched it anyway. I remembered telling India that it was based on a Shakespearean comedy but sitting there, my mind suddenly became blank and I couldn't recall the play. Since her death, I often have what I refer to as grief brain.

I walked over to the cabinet and chose my nail polish. I wanted a colour India would like. My choice: emerald green. She loved green and purple.

An older nail technician came over and turned on my massage chair. It felt good despite being mechanical and rough. She turned on the water in the footbath and sprinkled in some blue powder. It made the water look like a melted slushy. I placed my feet in it and sighed.

I pictured India over at the manicure station getting her fingernails buffed. The technicians loved her. "She's so beautiful," they'd cry. "So pretty." My belly would tighten with pride and sorrow. I used to believe I was slightly responsible for her beauty. But the recent months have taught me these things are a fluke, the result of some crazy genetic cake batter.

The technician returned and told me to take my right foot out of the water. She made no attempt to smile or chat. She wore blue surgical gloves. I remembered the box of gloves that were left in India's room after she died. Yolly, one of her home-care nurses, kept them next to the bottles of Ativan, morphine, and anti-psychotics. All those drugs I never imagined knowing about.

She began scraping my foot. Curls of skin lay on the towel like butter. Three women entered the spa. Even from a distance it was easy to tell they were family: a mother and her two grown-up daughters. As they were led to their chairs, I noticed the older-looking daughter was carrying a newborn in a car seat. I caught sight of its tiny foot and knew it was a girl.

The technician working on me turned to the mother and said, "You have a boy. A beautiful boy."

"She's a girl," the mother corrected.

"Ahhh ...," the technician said.

The mother sat in the massage chair next to mine and I peered down at the baby even though I knew I shouldn't. She reminded me of India. My heart was rattling inside me as if was a tin can filled with rusty nails. I wished I could bolt up from my chair and run all the way home. The assistant began scraping my other foot.

"What's her name?" I asked.

"Ella."

"She's beautiful," I said softly, afraid to speak too loudly. I was sure everyone in the spa could see my pain. I felt like Hester Prynne in *The Scarlet Letter*, my loss as obvious as the scarlet *A* pinned to Prynne's chest. The baby started to fuss, small mewing sounds then livid screams. My breasts ached as if it was my responsibility to feed her. Her mother got up and began to pace back and forth. She cooed and the baby fell back to sleep.

"How old is she?"

"Five weeks."

"It gets easier," I said, immediately regretting the remark. After my toenails were painted I decided to get my fingernails done. This way I'd be sitting with my back to the baby as my toenails dried. The baby began to cry again. In my head I repeated over and over, *She's hungry, she's hungry, she's hungry. Feed her.*

The nail technician nods towards my left hand, gesturing that I should put it in the bowl of warm water. Slow breaths, I tell myself. The technician taps the tattoo on my forearm, which reads "Stay Gold" with the dates of India's birth and death written under it.

"Why you do this?"

"It's for my daughter. She died."

"Oh no," she says. "This is very bad. This way you never forget."

Lady, I think, *do you really think I ever forget?* But I don't. There's no point. Instead I say, "I like it."

"You only have one child."

I nod. More than anything I want her to shut up.

"How old your daughter?"

"Sixteen."

I can hear the mother talking to her baby. "There, there," she purrs. I want to tell this mother that she's the luckiest woman in the world. Tell her I would do anything to go back in time. I don't.

My story would make her blood run cold.

I put my right hand in the bowl of water. I note the lines on my hands, wonder when this began happening. When did these wrinkles first appear? The last six months are a blur. It seems to me that one day I was forty-two, the next I was forty-eight, forty-nine, fifty-one. I've been robbed of years as well as of my daughter.

I don't remember my forties. I don't know how I will manage my fifties. Like Dorothy from *The Wizard of Oz*, one day I'm just home from school, the next I'm in the eye of a tornado. My whole life suddenly cyclonic.

Earlier in the day, my grief counsellor asked me to tell her about India. "Vain," I said. "Mark found 450 selfies on his computer."

"Wonderful."

"Crazy. This was a girl who couldn't feed herself but she managed to take all those selfies."

My counsellor has big blue eyes. I see them begin to water. "How lucky you are to have those."

"They're hard to look at."

"But, you have them."

The technician begins painting my nails with cuticle oil. She has cut my nails so they are short but elegant. "You're young, you can have more babies," she says factually rather than sympathetically.

"I'm too old – I can't. No more babies."

She puts down my hand and picks up my other hand. I wait for her to say something but she's silent. I'm grateful.

I'm never safe from grief. It finds me wherever I am. In the beginning it was advertisements. I never knew how many featured kids until after she was gone. Just the other day it was an ad for a movie about Stephen Hawking. People, especially young people in wheelchairs, are the hardest. A fellow student, a young woman in my MFA program, suffers from MS and is wheelchair-bound. Like India she has trouble using her arms and needs assistance to drink and eat. Though she doesn't look like India, I saw a similarity in the way she held herself and the shape of her chin. Sometimes I would find myself watching her. It was like I was playing a game of dare with myself. I felt awful. I was afraid she'd see me and think I was staring at her. But looking at her made me feel close to India. At the same time, watching her assistant feed her reminded me of all those months I fed India, believing that it was a temporary state that would soon get better.

One of the last places I expected to find grief was at my friend Lisa's sixtieth birthday party. I thought I would go and have a few drinks, see some friends. For her birthday Lisa had decided to have a bonfire and burn an effigy of herself. The effigy was beautiful – Lisa's an artist who makes sculptures with found objects. It was built with a wire armature, stuffed with straw, and filled with things she wanted to get rid of: old letters from mean lovers, rejection slips, old diaries, drawings she never finished.

When we got to the party it was in full swing. The bonfire was surrounded by people. There was whiskey and hot apple cider. I poured myself a huge glass of both. Lisa's two grown sons, who I've known since they were children, waved as they saw me. Her stepdaughter, who I'd also known as a child, came over and said hello.

The effigy was seated in an old wingback chair that she had stripped of upholstery. I thought it looked like a throne. The effigy slumped against the side of the chair, the way India often sat in her wheelchair. In the glow of the firelight, the effigy's face – a photocopy of a photograph of Lisa's face – looked a sickly yellow and sad.

Mark helped Lisa move the effigy into the fire. It licked the sides of the chair. The legs of the effigy caught the flames first. The fire slowly travelled up to the thighs and the core of its body. I thought about my daughter, how only a year ago I had chosen the clothes for my daughter to be cremated in: black jeans, a Japanese kimono dressing gown, her favourite quilt.

4

A Culture of Illness

O brave new world,
That has such people in't!
> – William Shakespeare
> *The Tempest, Act 5, Scene 1*

India's medical records from The Children's Hospital of Eastern Ontario (CHEO) are 513 pages long. I was once told that the average Canadian novel is 345 pages. The package was so heavy it was torn at the seams when it arrived. Originally I wasn't sure I'd have access to India's records. Parents aren't automatically approved for this, the information officer at the Office of the Information and Privacy Commissioner of Ontario told me. The Personal Health Information Protection Act states: "A health information custodian may disclose personal health information about an individual who is deceased, or is reasonably suspected to be deceased, to the spouse, partner, sibling or child of the individual if the recipients of the information reasonably require the information to make decisions about their own health care or their children's health care."

The officer advised me to write a letter to the Manager of Health Records at CHEO, explaining that I needed the records in order to, in their words, "find closure." She wasn't sure if it would work, but it was all she could suggest.

I once imagined the records as a long highway of facts stretching towards a definitive conclusion. In reality they are more like an old maple tree, the kind India would've once tried to climb, each new symptom a branch, determining its own direction.

The records sat in a drawer for several weeks. Finally, Mark organized them for me, dividing them into six sections, by date, from 2007 to 2013, one for each year of her illness. We've made two copies of each bundle. I put these in two big binders. Both are covered with a patchwork of fluorescent Post-it Notes.

Our version of the records begins in 2007, with our first trip to the ER.

When I started writing eighteen years ago, the Chekhovian gun theory was my motto. "Remove everything that has no relevance to the story. If you say in the first chapter that there is a rifle hanging on the wall, in the second or third chapter it absolutely must go off. If it's not going to be fired, it shouldn't be hanging there."

Reading the medical records is reminiscent of this theory, not because of what they have unnecessarily included, but for what they leave out. To me, they are like an Egyptian mummy: a dried husk with its organs removed and placed in canopic jars. Only instead of leaving the heart intact – the Egyptians believed this to be centre of a person's intelligence and understanding – it too has been removed. And the flesh of the story has been scraped away.

When I told my friends I was going to read the records, they warned me it was going to be hard. I shrugged this off. All in all, I reasoned, they wouldn't tell me anything I didn't know. This was a story I'd lived.

This remains true. They offer no insights. What I wasn't prepared for, though, is that with each document I'm propelled back in time. I'd almost forgotten the healthy girl who, before August 2007, had only visited the hospital two or three times for minor and ordinary childhood accidents. She'd been eclipsed by the failing India of the hospital years.

From August 2007 to October 2013, India was seen by twenty-five doctors in a diverse range of fields including Neurology, Neuropsychology, Genetics, Adolescent Medicine, and many others.

These doctors treated my family with respect and kindness. There was one exception, a neurologist from Sick Kids, who became offended when I asked if he'd ever seen any case like India's before. Afterwards, I was informed by our social worker that he probably felt I should have asked permission from India's neurologist before seeking his opinion. I'd made a breach of protocol. My fault.

India was treated by an army of nurses. I wish I remembered all their names.

They were the ones who helped me ford my way through the system. Above all, three nurses stand out: a male nurse who played music and got India and her roommate to dance (a considerable accomplishment considering India's roommate was completely immobile and would just lie on her bed shaking to the music); a nurse from the oncology ward who allowed me to keep a contraband kettle in the room and entertained India with her world travels; and the nurse who was caring for India the day she had a six-minute seizure. She called the Spot Team immediately and afterwards told me it was the scariest moment of her twenty-year nursing career.

During the first four years of India's illness I was contacted by a social worker three times. The first time was on the phone in February 2010, three years after she became sick. The notes describe me voicing my concern for India's quality of life and for my own. It states that I ask about support groups for parents to which it was recommended I go online. The social worker writes that she offered to meet with me, and that I declined (which I do not recall). She also states that she intended to maintain phone contact. It wasn't until two years later that I heard from her again. We then met twice to discuss the best way to get information from doctors. After this, our neighbourhood Centre Local de Services Communautaires (CLSC) was contacted and they sent a social worker to help us navigate the Quebec system. She was emotionally available and dedicated. Sadly, though, she was replaced by another who, while perfectly adequate, was not as intuitive.

There are forty-one clinical notes and twenty-six letters from her two main neurologists, Dr. Humphries and Dr. Sell, to India's family doctor and the doctors to whom she was referred. These, along with the discharge notes from her many hospital stays, are the backbone of India's medical history.

The clinical reports include the results of her many electroencephalograms (EEGs). The format is simple, with headings such as Object, Technical Information, Description, Impression, and Classification. At the end of each is the neurologist's name and the date it was transcribed. The first, on August 20, 2007, is remarkable only for its optimism. Under the heading of Impression, the neurologist hypothesizes that the diagnosis will likely be a juvenile epilepsy and that the "maintained background activity would be against a progressive epilepsy syndrome. Clinical correlation, however, would be necessary." Six years later, her last EEG tells a vastly different story: "This is a markedly abnormal EEG due to the presence of semi-continuous generalized epileptic form activity, in keeping with this patient's underlying diagnosis of progressive myoclonic epilepsy."

If I were to anthropomorphize a disease, India's would be The Trickster. A staple of all cultures, The Trickster is known for harbouring secret knowledge, using it to play tricks, and refusing to obey the rules – a shape-shifter like Loki, of Viking mythology, one moment appearing as some tameable creature, the next an engineer of death.

I read the letters from India's two neurologists hoping they'd reveal an aspect of her disease I'd missed. They didn't. What I did discover surprised me. Both doctors describe India's intelligence and her sense of irony (they weren't the only physicians to do this; it's a consistent feature throughout the records). At first read this might easily be construed to have been an aside. In truth, it wasn't. It was this single fact, her continued high level of intelligence, that confounded them over the course of her treatment. All the diseases for which they considered India to have been a candidate were marked by intellectual decline. But year after year, despite her physical decline, she continued to grow intellectually.

Still, these letters offered me little in the way of comfort. Although I was touched by both doctors' dedication to her cause and their concern for her well-being, I was astonished by how much of India's story was missing. While the early letters do specify bits and pieces about her education and her social life, there are only one or two observations about how India was coping emotionally and nothing at all about how Mark and I managed the rigours of her daily regime. It would appear these things were of no consequence – unless Mark and I brought them up.

She tried eighteen drugs for seizure control: Divalproex (Valproic Acid) – 2007; Lamotrigine – 2008; Lorazepam (Ativan) – 2008; Leviteracetam (Keppra) – 2009; Clonazepam – 2010; Acetazolamide – 2010; Ethosuximide (Zarontin) – 2010; MCT oil – 2010; Morphine (Statex) – 2010; Ortho-Evra – 2011; Diazepam (Valium) – 2011; Ondansetron (nausea) – 2011; Clobazam – 2012; Rufinamide – 2012; Depo-Provera – 2012; Primidone – 2012; Piracetam – 2012; and Methylprednisolone (Steroid) – 2013.

Each brought its own particular and brutal side effects:

suicidal thoughts, excess sleepiness, slurred speech, anger, and so on. One drug made her throw up so violently she began having symptoms of anorexia. These side effects not only hurt India physically but also psychologically. Often she acted out of character, her friends finding themselves hurt or surprised by her actions. At one point I would've said the drugs were useless. Often I felt they made her sicker. I wrote on my blog in 2011 that "before each appointment, I'd tell myself if he (her neurologist) suggests another drug I'll say no. But we were so desperate I caved every time." I began my blog "Fall On Me, Dear" in order to find answers for these kinds of questions. And though this didn't happen, I found a supportive audience from across the world, who often shared their own stories with me.

From 2007 to 2013, we made eighty-four phone calls to the Neurology Department. I thought there would be more, but Mark reminded me that we only tended to call when we were really worried. One feature of our lives clearly demonstrated in these notes is how often the three of us were forced to adapt to the *New Normal*, or, as it's referred to in medical jargon, the *New Baseline*. This was constantly changing. In the early years, the New Normal meant, simply, that since India now took medicine daily she would have to be supervised while swimming. Several years later it meant that her hands shook so badly that in the mornings I had to dress her for school. This could take up to an hour; a fashionista, India was rarely content with my suggestions.

It never occurred to me that these adjustments were permanent – I saw them as temporary, to be endured and overcome. I believed it was only a matter of time before a solution was found. Maybe I was purposely naïve, but I don't think so. I never expected her to get worse. The doctors never led us to believe she would either, though looking back, I'm not sure they really understood what we were up against.

Our calls are recorded in the Interdisciplinary Telephone Log, which details the date, the reason for the call, who called, the assessment, the advice given, the prescription, the follow-up, and the duration of the call. The average length of the call was ten minutes. The most common reason for them was that the newest drug, or cocktail of drugs, had stopped working, and she was again seizing frequently or falling over. They are an unrelenting indicator of how the disease took its toll on her physically.

In the beginning, there are messages about her being shaky but later they note the difficulty of bringing India into CHEO for her appointments because of the anxiety it caused her to be moved. By then, she was completely reliant on us. She could no longer stand or walk, the movement of her arms and hands limited.

As the disease progressed Mark was forced to carry her through the house – to the toilet, to her bedroom, to the living room. In doing this, Mark shared a physical intimacy fathers of teenage girls rarely do. She'd wrap her arms tight around his neck and cling to him. Our beloved house was suddenly alive with danger: our claw-foot bathtub a reminder that she could drown, the hardwood floors too slippery. Even eating became dangerous: the cutlery, the glasses, the hot steaming food.

Several times a day he'd carry her down the steep staircase to the living room. Not an easy task. By then she was five foot four, and a hundred and thirty pounds. I'd watch from the bottom of the stairs, as he slowly made his way, one step after another, the stairs under his feet narrow and worn.

India hated the stairs. He'd have to reassure her as they made their way down. Recently Mark told me that when we first viewed our house, the old stairway was one of the features he liked immediately. His feelings have altered dramatically since then. In some ways he hates them. They are a poignant reminder of his daughter's physical decline. Yet he remembers India telling him she liked the fact that she got to hug him when he carried her down.

I couldn't lift India. So when Mark wasn't home, I'd get her to lie on a blanket and I'd drag her gently. The wheelchair was too large to maneuver through the hallways of our house. Sometimes I'd sit her on Mark's office chair and push her where she wanted to go. This was problematic. India had a tendency to fall forward, so I had to wrap my arms around her shoulders and push at the same time. If she wanted the toilet or a bath, it took all my strength to hold her or pull her up. She used to get impatient with me but eventually after a struggle, we'd manage it. As I couldn't carry her down the stairs, my method was to seat her in front of me, secure her with my legs, and hold her around the waist, while we thumped slowly down each stair on our bottoms. When we finally reached the end I'd pull her up and, as quickly as I could, half drag her to the sofa. Once there she'd lie, her head propped up with pillows, and watch an episode of *Dr. Phil*.

There are thirty-nine emails from Mark and me in the records, mostly from 2011 to 2013. They have subject lines like Grand Mal, The State of India, and India's Condition. The early emails are relatively benign. There are questions about medications and dosages, questions about side effects, and questions about the MCT oil diet.

The MCT oil diet is a variant of the ketogenic diet, known to control seizures, a regime of medium-chain triglycerides that strictly limits the intake of carbohydrates and requires the patient to take a shot glass full of oil six times a day, at two-hour intervals, so that their brain is starved of sugars and forced to survive on the fat. We tried this for a year and a half. In theory the diet would replace India's medications. This didn't entirely work in her case. She remained throughout on one drug: Keppra.

India was fourteen when we travelled to Sick Kids to begin the diet treatment. The dietician and I were polar opposites. She believed in the strictest adherence to the dietary rules. Once, unaware that the oil had to be stored in glass, I bought plastic containers and was told off so severely that I felt she believed I'd done it on purpose.

Before she and I met, Mark, who had travelled to Sick Kids previously with India, had tried to explain to the dietician that I wasn't good with rules. I was upset with Mark about this: I believed it created an awkward dynamic between the dietician and me. Later, when the diet stopped working, I felt she blamed my administering of it, rather than consider that it may have been the wrong treatment entirely. Naturally there's no way for me to confirm this, and I'm aware my feelings could be incorrect.

The rules of the diet reminded me of a method I'd used at Weight Watchers. The problem was the book containing India's food allowances only listed traditional foods. For example, the only flour listed was white. There was no information about other low-carb options, like almond or coconut. I could sense the dietician was wary about anything not listed. When I finally asked her about this, she gave me a funny look and told me that not many of the children on the program had mothers who baked or cooked. She considered it commendable that I did.

The other impediment was that the dietician seemed to have little appreciation of what it was like to be on this diet from a practical or emotional viewpoint. She talked to India as if she was a dull five-year-old and not a perceptive teenage girl, a teenager who'd spent enough time with medical experts that she often knew more about the effects of the medicines they prescribed than they did.

When the dietician told India about the oil she said it would come in a milkshake, so we both envisioned a fluffy, fruit-flavoured, sugar-free, milk-based drink. In reality, it was a quarter cup of milk and oil, shaken together by hand, in a plastic bottle. The dietician said the oil was tasteless. I doubt she'd ever actually tasted it. The few times I drank it, it made my mouth feel thick and bitter like when I was catching a cold.

The typical dose was thirty grams, the equivalent of enough olive oil to make two family-sized salad dressings. At night I would weigh the oil and pour it into small glass jam jars for the next day. I was constantly trying to find ways to make the oil more palatable. This was challenging. It had the consistency and stickiness of baby oil, and it couldn't be heated so I couldn't use it to bake with.

I tried hiding it in India's food, dribbling it into a meat sauce or blending it with a carb-free Caesar dressing. But it didn't mix well, and she'd always discover it and refuse to eat her meal. Now and then I would find something that worked for a while. Through research I learned that Knox's gelatin was carb-free so I created a pudding, combining the oil, Watkin's flavoured extracts – usually vanilla or caramel – and her milk allotment. Eventually she grew tired of the texture. Then I bought a small ice cream maker and used the same ingredients to make a frozen version. This worked for a month or so. After that, I tried blending it with yogurt, then soft tofu, even herbal tea. Nothing lasted.

Wherever she went she had to take the oils with her. In the morning when she went to school she took three portions. These were seldom finished. As soon as she arrived home from school she took another. A special event, like a three-day trip to Upper Canada Village with her home school group, meant preparing eighteen portions in advance – in addition to all her meals.

Her meals were a challenge too. A typical carb allowance was about half a slice of bread. I'd buy French bread and cut it as thinly as I could in order to make it look as if she had a larger portion. At each meal she was allowed a small amount of fruit or vegetables. The only vegetable she was allowed to have in abundance was iceberg lettuce. If she wanted chili, or another meal that combined meat and vegetables, I would have to make her portion separately, weighing each ingredient, trying to decide which were the most essential to the meal. The only meals we ever had out were at the Korean BBQ house. Her protein allowance was so liberal she could practically eat her weight in meat. We only had to be careful about any sauces. Her rice allowance was the size of a small sushi roll.

The diet worked at first, though she didn't look healthy. At five foot three, she dropped to about eighty pounds and wore a size zero. Her skin was ashen. She moved like a marionette being controlled by a toddler, continually on the verge of toppling over.

Much of the correspondence during this period focuses on the side effects of the diet. India developed kidney stones. In order to control the pain she took morphine. This made her constipated, which increased her pain. A vicious cycle evolved. For this reason, and others, she became increasingly resistant to drinking the oil. Some days it could take up to three hours to convince her to take one portion. This meant the schedule was thrown off and we'd have to wake her up at night to give her the final dose.

Days were divided into two-hour segments. Either she was due to take an oil or she'd just taken one. Whenever I knew she was due to take an oil, I would be flooded with anxiety. I knew there was no way I could make her if she wasn't willing and I believed – perhaps because I had to – that this treatment was the only option when it came to making her well. Sometimes if India's best friend, Ally, was visiting, she could get her to take the oil. India didn't mind this as much. I was always grateful to Ally for this little break. Like me, Ally used to try to convince India to gulp it down quickly and get it over with. She never would.

One episode in particular stands out in my mind. It was a Saturday, late in the afternoon. Mark, India, and I were huddled in the bathroom, India sitting on the floor, leaning against the toilet. She'd just taken a bath and was behind three doses. Mark and I were pleading with her to take the oil. I was so frustrated I was crying. Suddenly I slapped her across the face. She didn't cry. Instead she just glared at me, her green eyes fiery with hatred. Of course, she still refused to drink the oil.

I had to leave the room. Leave Mark to deal with her. Later that day, I remember begging her to forgive me. I'd never lost control with my child like that before. I loathe physical discipline. I think she might have laughed and said that she hated me. She liked to tease me. I can't forgive myself for this. Mark says India forgave me. Still, I can't let go.

After India went off the diet, I often thought about writing the dietician. I wanted to tell her what it was like to administer the diet and how it affected us as a family. Like most of what we went through in our travels through the system, no attention was given to our family's emotional well-being. Nobody ever considered how we coped. I'm not sure why this is.

My theory is that many of the people who treated India simply didn't understand what it was like to be sick or what it's like to be a family caregiver. Many were so engrossed by the science of the disease they forgot there was a person behind the symptoms. Now and again I like to daydream that the dietician is my patient for a day. I imagine talking to her the way she spoke to India.

There were six ambulance rides in total. Three fifteen-minute rides from our home to the local hospital in Wakefield then three forty-five-minute rides from there to CHEO in Ottawa. There's even one flight, when she was transported from CHEO to Sick Kids in Toronto. Thankfully, the Emergency Department records do not show the times I snapped at the ER doctor or the nurse in admitting. They do, however, detail that Mark and I were both frequently at her bedside, and considered "reliable" when it came to describing our daughter's symptoms.

India never paid much attention to her hospital room-mates. When she wasn't sleeping, she tended to put on her headphones to watch a movie and escape. She hardly ever ventured to the activity room despite the insistence of the cheery volunteers. Only once do I remember her going enthusiastically. She was enticed by the sight of a rather dreamy seventeen-year-old male volunteer.

She did love getting visitors, though. When they came she was the life of the party, brimming with energy and hu-mour. But as soon as they left, I'd watch her slowly retract back into the shell of her illness.

One of India's roommates – I'll call her Bella – still stands out in my mind. They shared a room on the fourth floor that would've otherwise been allotted to four patients, had the ward not been exceptionally quiet. The first time I noticed her it was mid-afternoon and the room was flooded with sunlight and she was fast asleep. She looked like a porcelain doll.

Her mother told me she was recovering from pneumo-nia after being in a coma for almost three weeks. Bella could barely lift her head and only communicated in moans. At night, her mother crawled into bed with her. All day long, her father sat stroking her hair.

The little kitchenette, no matter what ward we were on, was where the mothers of the hospital regulars met. Hospital moms were usually overweight or underweight – very few of us looked fit. We'd chat, reheat meals, pour glasses of water, boil water in the microwave – on the fourth floor the rumour was that there'd been a kettle, but it had been stolen – maybe we'd even make a date for a contraband glass of wine up in the parents' lounge, though that was rare. Most of us didn't dare leave our children's bedsides. We'd lean against the counter, keeping one eye on their doors and talk openly about failed treatments, drugs, doctors, and the system. With these mothers I could be comfortable. Nobody ever asked me how India was doing in school. They understood that sort of thing was the least of our worries.

What the medical file doesn't record is the financial challenges of having a chronically ill child. Illness is an expensive business, even with universal health care. It's fraught with hidden costs. Take parking, for example. During India's longest hospital stay, parking cost us over $200. This was with a discount card. The regular rate would have been $611. We only found out about the card by accident. The hospital administration seemed to assume everybody knew. Of course, a hospital stay also meant meals from the cafeteria. We tried to be organized, but some days we just couldn't make it to the supermarket.

Mark had to work when he wasn't with India. We were, and still are, self-employed, so we had no safety net. In the years we lived in Quebec, most of India's meds were covered but there were several that weren't. I don't know how we did it, but I remember scraping together $800 for a month's supply of one of these drugs, only to discover it didn't work.

When India first started having seizures, Mark ran a graphic design studio with three employees, but as the illness progressed he was forced to shut down his Ottawa studio, lay off his employees, and work from home in order to help with her care. This meant not only did our earnings decrease, but his workday was continuously being interrupted. He was often forced to work nights in order to keep up.

But Mark's business wind-down is not mentioned in the file; neither is the shift in my employment. For fourteen years, I'd run my own travelling theatre program for youth. I travelled around Ottawa and western Quebec teaching over a hundred students a year. It was impossible to continue as India's conditioned worsened, and not just because of the workload. I loved my students but I began to feel bitter being with them. It was like being forced to watch an old lover kissing his new girlfriend. We needed money, though, so I continued working part-time at a friend's yarn shop. This was easier to manage as I could always cancel a shift if India needed me. My co-workers knew about India and the stress we were under, and were supportive. They knew I seldom called in unless I had no other choice.

Throughout those years, it was the psychological repercussions that took the greatest toll, not just on India but on Mark and me as well. The disease continuously evolved. There were so many different types of seizures: drop attacks, drop attacks with eye-rolling, absences, absences coupled with head-drops, tonic-clonics, myoclonic absences, myoclonic jerks. In addition, she had difficulty with walking (ultimately she would be wheelchair-bound and bedridden), with hearing and processing sounds, with speaking and singing and with her fine motor skills. With each new symptom, we grew more afraid.

Even before I knew India would die, I grieved. Watching her as she got sicker and her abilities were more and more constrained, it was impossible not to recall proudly watching her attain her important childhood milestones – often long ahead of her contemporaries. At her toddler's gymnastic class she'd nimbly walked across the balance beam while her contemporaries still clutched their mothers' hands. Now, I watched the process reverse, as she lost skills she'd once so easily grasped.

I didn't know what to say when India asked me why she couldn't walk. "Why is this happening?" she once asked. "I used to be normal." If there'd been a reliable diagnosis it might've been easier. At least I'd have had an answer. Theories abounded but nothing fit. All I could tell her was that I didn't know, but that the doctors were working hard to find out. In hindsight I wonder what she thought of that. Did she still have faith in them or, like Mark and me, had she begun to doubt?

During the progression of her illness she was diagnosed with six epilepsies: Childhood Absence; Juvenile Absence; Juvenile Myoclonic Absence; Myoclonic Absence; and Subcortical Myoclonus (in addition to Myoclonic Absence).

She tested negative for severe epilepsies like Lennox-Gastaut, her condition sharing many similarities with a range of these very serious seizure disorders but having none of the mental deterioration or nocturnal seizure activity that's associated with almost all of them. Unusual also was the relatively late start to her illness, since some begin even before birth. She tested negative, as well, for a host of progressive syndromes such as Dravets, Unverrecht-Lundborg, and Lafora, the latter the disease that terrified me the most, as it is associated with dementia and hallucinations.

The records remind me there were tests for mitochondrial disorders: Rasmussen's Syndrome and Ring Chromosome 20. There were CT scans in 2007 and 2010, MRI's in 2007 and 2012, a bone marrow extraction testing for Neuronal Ceroid Lipofuscinosis in 2012, Genetic testing in 2011 for EPM1, EPM2A and B, MERF, and FEFHC1 (JME) as well as DRPL. It is an alphabet soup of disorders I can no longer remember the distinguishing features of, just that each possible diagnosis held out the hope of a solution and the fear of a sentence.

We were at the point where we'd eliminated all the tests that CHEO could offer us when in 2012 she underwent something called a Neuronal Ceroid-Lipofuscinoses (NCL) mutation panel and a complete gene sequencing which finally resulted in an answer. It took eight months to get the results. They revealed that India had an autosomal recessive genetic anomaly, two separate defects in subunit B of the ASAH1 gene, responsible for the production of Acid Ceramidase. Her physicians named it PME-SMA: Progressive Myoclonic Epilepsy with Spinal Muscular Atrophy. A one-of-a-kind disorder, with no other example in the world, but with similarities to another related ultra-rare genetic condition: Spinal Muscular Atrophy with Progressive Myoclonic Epilepsy (SMA-PME) – a disease so rare only a half-dozen or so cases exist in the world today. There was no treatment and no cure. The news was unimaginable and impossible for me to comprehend. How could India be dying from a disease nobody had ever heard of? How could she be one in seven billion? The file holds no answer to that, the most important question of all.

5

Home

Toto did not really care whether he was in Kansas or the Land of Oz so long as Dorothy was with him.

– L. Frank Baum
The Wonderful Wizard of Oz

The 150-year-old house stood across from the only inter-section in the village of Lascelles. One road led towards a turn-of-the-century red brick church, the other down a hilly road, past farmers' fields towards the town of Rupert. Both led towards graveyards, but I didn't notice that then. It was June, and wildflowers skirted the road. Everything was lush and green. We spotted the For Sale sign and drove care-fully up the wooded drive. A row of cedars stood around the house as if on guard.

India was sleeping on the back seat as she often did when we went for a drive. I don't know if she was even aware of us stopping. Mark and I got out of the car and sur-veyed the house.

The green paint was weathered and chipping. We could hear the sound of a tinkling bell from the door of the neigh-bouring shop. The grass was trimmed and well-tended. Stairs flanked by two crumbling stone walls led up the hill to the top of the property. I imagined a younger India running up them, eager to explore the hilly pasture.

The realtor pulled up in his worn Subaru. He shook our hands and motioned to the house, "Would you like to go inside?"

Mark opened the car door and told India we were going inside. She nodded sleepily at him, too tired to really take in what he was saying. She never seemed to get enough sleep; the drugs wore her out, though they did nothing to relieve the seizures that grew more frequent and severe. Sometimes she had trouble keeping her hands from shaking and the falls – the first sign we'd had that she was ill – still came without warning.

Whenever Mark or I walked anywhere with her, we kept ourselves at the ready, in case we had to catch her. It made me feel powerless. There was nothing I could do to protect her. At thirteen, India would refuse to let us walk with our arms around her, fighting continually for her independence. I did my best to respect this, but it was challenging. When I walked beside her, every muscle in my body tensed. Watching her play with friends, I had to fight the urge to shadow her. Occasionally when Mark was with her, he'd insist she let him hold her. She'd balk, then relent. But I knew she resented it. Recently we had borrowed an old pink wheelchair from a friend for her. She hated it.

I thought India looked like Clara, from the old black and white version of *Heidi* I'd seen as a kid. Thin and birdlike, she was no longer the robust child she'd been. I spent a lot of my time dreaming that, like Clara, we'd one day see her run and climb the way she had.

Not long before the trip to Lascelles, we'd received word that India had tested negative for a series of progressive epilepsies with strange unpronounceable names. I'd never heard of these diseases before. The symptoms were cruel and inexorable: intractable seizures, dementia, blindness, cognitive decline. In all of them the outcome was the same – death.

The three of us had met with the geneticists at CHEO before these tests. They were different from the other doctors. They asked questions about our family history. Did we have any ancestors from Scandinavia or the Baltic regions of Europe? Where did our ancestors emigrate from? Did any of our other relatives have seizures? It reminded me of visiting Hadrian's Wall as a child and watching the archaeologists dig: the measured slow process of excavation, of recording the past in order to understand the future.

I admired these doctors' intelligence and patience. I believed if the results of their tests were negative then it only made sense that India's illness was just a glitch. Soon things would get better. Her neurologist just hadn't found the right medication, or maybe her teenage hormones were interfering with the results. Eventually the mystery would be solved. India would be cured.

At the same time, I had a sense India's illness was not ordinary. Both Mark and I spent hours scouring the Internet, hoping to find some treatment or clue about her condition. We watched videos of other children with seizures, perused descriptions of all kinds of epilepsies, and read letters by parents who worried because their children had twenty or thirty seizures a day. Meanwhile our daughter's seizures were so frequent we lost count, yet nobody in the Neurology Department seemed as concerned as we were. I couldn't understand why.

The realtor led us up the veranda. The outside walls were covered with vintage metal signs of movies and classic 1950s European advertisements for grocery stores. The large front window looked into a generous living room with hardwood floors. The front door was painted red. My favourite colour.

I liked the house already but told myself not to get attached. When we'd begun looking at houses in the Wakefield area,

Mark and I had decided we'd make a sensible decision. No more old houses. Mark was adamant. This time we'd pick something practical. We'd chosen Wakefield as it was an area we'd long been attracted to. The atmosphere of the town was artistic and accepting. Both India and I had friends there. And Mark could be in the city for work in an hour.

The front room was large with high ceilings. Light spilled from the two large windows that dominated the space. The boards of the hardwood floor were thin and scratched. A steep staircase with a long banister and narrow worn stairs led to the second floor. Upstairs, there were three bedrooms, all with slanted ceilings and antique light fixtures and wooden doors with their original doorknobs.

The realtor led us from room to room, not saying much. The house reminded me of a British cottage, the kind found in the small village in the northeast of England where my grandma was from. The kind of place some working-class character from a Philippa Gregory novel would've grown up in. I was determined not to give in to the house's charm.

I wandered back downstairs and stood in the living room, watching the sunlight flicker against the walls as Mark inspected the stone basement.

He came back upstairs and touched my shoulder. "I want it, don't you?"

"Yes," I nodded. "I do."

I'd never expected to look for a house in the country. A confirmed city slicker, I loved being surrounded by people and the noise of urban life. Before my marriage I'd lived in London, England, and Sydney, Australia. I equated the country with boredom.

Hintonburg, the inner-city Ottawa suburb we lived in, had changed. When we'd first moved there it had a reputation for being rough, but that had never bothered me. I liked that the area had history and that my neighbours were as diverse as the old red brick mansions that lined the avenues. But it was now the trendiest neighbourhood in the city and many of our original neighbours had fled. Our once quiet street was now packed with cars and the neighbours who'd remained were renovating. In the past this wouldn't have bothered me, but faced with the everyday traumas of trying to care for India, whenever I left my house I felt shocked by the noise and the optimism of the world.

But this country home felt right; it was the kind of place I imagined India one day bringing her children to visit. A home that would look fine covered in signs that read *Grandma's Place* or *Greatest Grandma Ever.*

CHEO served the Western Quebec region so India could continue her treatment, and though we didn't discover this until after we moved, her medication would also be covered.

We were busy preparing for our move to the country when a friend called to tell me she'd been to a wedding in Toronto and bumped into a high school friend who was a pediatric neurologist in the States. "You have to take India to see Dr. Snead at Sick Kids in Toronto," she said.

Finally, I thought, we're going to get some answers. I'd been trying for months to get India a meeting with the dietician at CHEO. I'd read on the Internet about the ketogenic diet, a high-fat diet that successfully treated intractable seizures. I believed it was the cure for India. But when I talked about it with our neurologist, Dr. Humphries, he was non-committal, saying they rarely advised it for children over twelve. It was too difficult to administer.

I thought it would be easy to get a referral to Sick Kids. We'd just tell Dr. Humphries and we'd be on our way. But we had to push. Something about us going to Toronto made Humphries nervous. I couldn't put my finger on why. Surely it was clear we needed a second opinion.

Eventually we were given the referral, and we scraped together the money for Mark and India to fly to Toronto. By this point, any extra money we had was being used to pay for India's drugs. Some months we spent close to a thousand dollars. Because we were both self-employed, we covered the cost ourselves. Once or twice Mark's parents paid. Finally, we received some funds from the Trillium Foundation. This was calculated on a yearly basis so we had to pay upfront before we received a small grant.

In Toronto Dr. Snead gave India a new diagnosis: a rare but not unheard of form of epilepsy called Juvenile Epilepsy. He agreed she should be on the ketogenic diet. A report was sent that day to the neurology clinic in Ottawa. Suddenly, things started to change. We were told India would be admitted into CHEO to be weaned off her medications and begin the diet. We were due to move into the house in two and half weeks. The timing was awkward but we didn't dare miss this opportunity. We would make it work.

On the day of India's admittance, we arrived promptly. India was given a bed on the fourth floor in a room with two beds. I don't remember the other patient. Over the years, India shared rooms with so many sick children that I've lost track of them except for the really sick or unusual. I remember it seemed as if we waited for hours before Neurology contacted us.

Finally, Dr. Humphries arrived and led Mark and me into a small conference room. I remember watching Dr. Humphries change the tag on the door so it said occupied and being afraid. This was the first time Mark and I had been led into a small room. I didn't know the significance at the time. Dr. Humphries quickly told us that the dietician had refused to take India's case. I never learned the reason why but I remember I was shocked to learn that could happen. India would be flown to Sick Kids to undergo treatment there. She would be there two weeks.

The three of us waited for hours for India to be airlifted from CHEO to Sick Kids. In that time, Mark and I decided, he would go the first week and I would stay and pack. We would switch the following week so he would be home for the move.

That night after they left, I began packing the basement. To alleviate my worry as I packed, I watched episodes of *Sex and the City*. The vapid predictability of the characters' lives calmed me. If I was worried, I distracted myself with Carrie's romances and all those glorious shoes.

By the end of the week, when I boarded the midnight bus to Toronto for my turn at the hospital, much of the house was packed. I was nervous, not sure how India would be when I arrived. They were weaning her off the drugs. Mark warned me that the doctors expected she'd seize badly. The dietician was starting her on the MCT oil diet. Despite my fear, I fell asleep quickly across two seats, my legs bridging the aisle.

I arrived at Sick Kids as morning was breaking. It was like entering a futuristic set from *Logan's Run* with its glass elevators and large domed ceiling. I half-expected Michael York to run in, followed by a scantily clad Jenny Agutter. In comparison, CHEO looked like a hospital from the Depression era, with its clanking elevators and low ceilings.

India was sleeping in her room on the fourth floor. I kissed her cheek and told her I loved her. She looked better than I'd imagined. There was colour in her cheeks. I sat down on the sofa bed near her and guarded over her.

A week later, India and I joined Mark in our new house. The feeling of optimism that had begun in the entrance hall of Sick Kids followed me to our new home. India still slept a great deal but this was to be expected in the early weeks of the treatment. Her body was adjusting to the regime. I saw positive signs. She was less shaky, more talkative, and involved in life again. It could take up to a year for the seizures to completely disappear, the team at Sick Kids said.

I allowed myself to envision a normal life for India. I saw her riding horses in the neighbouring fields, walking in the woods, jumping in the river with her long-legged teenaged friends. Maybe one day, I imagined, India would get married here. A country wedding complete with camping and singing around the bonfire. I'd found my perfect fairy-tale cottage of happy endings.

It was all going to be okay.

But it wasn't.

India never even walked the entire property. Instead of our life in the city becoming a chapter we looked back at as something we endured and survived, it would become the fairy tale. My new dream home became the witch's house from "Hansel and Gretel," the bubbling cauldron a symbol of the mutated genes percolating in my daughter.

I didn't want to get out of bed but I forced myself to get up. This wasn't unusual. In the two years since India's death I constantly struggled with getting out of bed. Mark and I were in Penticton, British Colombia, staying at an Airbnb rental that faced Lake Skaha. The lake was so vast it reminded me of the Mediterranean, the massive unending blue of the lake meeting the sky. I wanted to stay but we were heading home to Quebec. I couldn't eat. I wanted to, but when I tried my stomach tensed and tightened. When I did manage to eat, I cried afterwards, as if my grief was some mythological beast that woke when it was fed.

I went down to the beach and sat in the sun and smoked a cigarette. It was deserted despite the warmth of the April air. An elderly lady walked by. She was petite with high cheekbones and fine white hair cut elegantly around her face. She was beautiful in a way that I found encouraging. I was turning fifty in a month and I felt in the aftermath of India's death that I looked much older than my years.

I couldn't figure out how old the woman was but I'd been watching her all week as she took her daily walk. She moved very slowly. My guess was she was at least eighty.

I decided to say hello. A friend from Penticton had told me I'd have to become friendlier if I wanted to become a local. "It's such a beautiful day," I said.

"Yes," she agreed.

"I can't get over it. I'm from the Ottawa area."

"Oh, my daughter works there. It's cold," she said. "Do you have any children?"

"No." I paused. "Do you have a big family?" I asked, hoping to distract her.

"I have four children – three sons." She paused and cleared her throat. "My youngest son and my granddaughter died ten years ago in a car crash. Up there." She pointed to the nearby mountains.

"I'm so sorry. I lost my daughter. That's why I'm here."

"Funny," she said. "I never tell anyone. I guess I was supposed to meet you. Only someone who's been through it understands. This month is always difficult for me. It's the anniversary."

"October for me. My daughter would've been eighteen in May. It's only been eighteen months."

"Oh, that's still so new. How are you doing?"

"I'm supposed to go home and I don't want to. I can't eat. I can't stand the idea of being in my house."

She moved towards me and hugged me. "You can move. You don't have to stay there."

We walked a little way up the road together then stopped. "My name's Lesley," I said.

"I'm Joan." She paused, looked down on the ground. "Do you believe in God? I don't mean that in a funny way. It's just my faith really helps me."

"Not in a traditional sense. I don't really pray in the real way. Just sort of talk to India."

"I don't think God really cares about religion," Joan said.

"Neither do I."

"I'm glad I met you, Lesley. You made my day."

"Me too. Thank you for understanding." She hugged me again, there in the middle of the road.

"Maybe we'll see each other again before I leave. I'll look out for you."

"Do," she said, beginning to make her way down the road. I stood and watched as she disappeared onto the path into the park.

Joan had confirmed what I'd already suspected. Mark and I could no longer live in our house. We were done with Quebec and our lives there. Our winter house-sitting for my parents in Gibsons, British Columbia, had taught us that while we couldn't escape our grief, it was easier in a place without memories, especially if that place was warm. The cold of the Quebec winters seemed to add an extra bitterness to our condition. We were both scared as we set off back to our old home. From time to time, one of us would ask the other, "We don't have to stay, right?" The answer was always the same, "No, we're not staying." We took turns reassuring each other.

Back in Wakefield I was hesitant to tell my friends I was moving. Earlier in the year, when I'd mentioned it to an acquaintance – another bereaved mother – she'd accused me of wanting to run away. "You can't run from grief," she said.

Her words had annoyed me. It was impossible for me to imagine we could have a new life if we stayed in our house and lived in a community where I'd see my daughter's friends grow up. We could never escape the past and we didn't want to. I thought about my daughter constantly. I knew it was the same for Mark. But we owed to ourselves a chance of survival. How would that be possible if we were continually assaulted with memories and associations? Why is it bad to run away? I thought to myself. If I was being chased by a bear, I'd run. Nobody would expect me to fight the bear.

Unlike my imaginary bear, I knew the grief would follow me. But at least, in a new place, I believed I could find some respite: a range of mountains to gaze at; a beach to walk; the big open British Columbia sky, where I liked to imagine India riding her spirit horse.

Once back in Wakefield we drove straight to Una's house, fifteen minutes from our house, set high on hills overlooking the Gatineau River. It was Una's suggestion we live with her. When she'd first suggested it, I hadn't been sure. Perhaps I was just being weak. But after travelling east across the States towards home, where every mile closer brought more tears and apprehension, I was certain of our decision. I might have forced myself to endure it in the past – might have even acted as if I didn't mind it or liked it, but I was discovering with grief one did a lot of pretending in public and I just didn't have the energy to do it in private as well. It was exhausting behaving normally.

The plan was, we'd pack up the house then rent it out. I'd work at Una's café for the summer and make some money. I'd worked for her on and off the summer before. Of course, I knew I'd see a lot of little girls in the café. But the average customer turnover was twenty-five minutes, so there wouldn't be much time to think.

Back in Wakefield the grief came back with a vengeance. It was as if the clock had been turned back. In the evenings, I sat out on the screened porch, crying, begging India to come home to me.

I felt very far away from India. Perhaps it was because I was slowly leaving the fog of deep grief, where the rational mind is so absent and the intuitive mind is in charge. When she'd first died, I felt that I heard from her all the time, that everywhere I looked I found evidence of her. Messages. Odd coincidences that made me feel as if we were still together. Some of these were simple things. I'd turn on my car radio and a song she used to sing would be playing. This might not have given me pause had her tastes been as pedestrian as any other sixteen-year-old's, but she had a taste for the esoteric. At eleven, while most of her peers at voice class sang Katie Perry hits, she favoured Fiona Apple and Barbara Streisand. The song I most associated with her was John

Cale's version of "Hallelujah," a rendition of the Leonard Cohen hit. She'd sung that song over and over again, trying to master it. Now, wherever I went, it seemed to follow me.

It wasn't just songs. Everywhere, I seemed to be followed by little girls. I was overwhelmed by them. The more I tried to avoid them, the closer they seemed to get. We'd go out to dinner and I'd find myself seated facing a three-year-old girl dressed in a tutu.

One day, while I was serving on the café's patio, I counted eleven girls in my section and only three boys. Each of these girls was a reminder of India. A teenager who couldn't decide between an ice coffee and a cappuccino, groaning at her mother's jokes. A tween, who'd insisted her mother take her out for an adventure. A five-year-old, who spoke with the eloquence of an educated adult. All aspects of my daughter.

Friends even began to notice them. "You just can't get away from them," Una said. "I think India's sending them."

"Well, if she is, I wish she'd stop."

"Maybe you need to acknowledge them," she said.

That sentiment was echoed by another friend. "Embrace the little girls. Embrace them," she said.

Then strangely the grief became more manageable. One afternoon I served a middle-aged couple sitting on the patio, and the woman kept smiling at me.

"I know you from somewhere," she said.

I didn't recognize her, but I diligently listed all the possibilities. No, none of these were it. Finally, I said, "I lived in the Hintonburg area for a long time. Where do you live?"

Ah, she said, that's it. I lived on Armstrong. Then she said, "Could it be I remember you going everywhere with a little blonde girl? You were both always chatting away."

"Yes," I said. "That was my daughter. She passed."

"I'm so sorry. You two had something special," she said. "I remember."

"My husband and I are moving to B.C. at the end of the summer. We can't stay here."

Her husband looked up at me. "I know something of loss. It's good you're leaving. Where are you going?"

"Penticton in the Okanagan Valley."

"I'm from Calgary. I know that area well. Things will be better for you there. It's beautiful."

Later I met up with the husband as he came up to pay his bill at the cash register. "It's going to be better out west," he said.

The way he spoke comforted me. I don't know why, maybe I just wanted to believe him.

"I know about loss," he repeated. "I lost my wife when my daughter was only two and my son was a baby. The woman with me is the only mother they've known. My kids are in their twenties. Things will get easier."

After work, I thought about that chance meeting. How those many years ago, India and I had been wandering around Hintonburg, lost in our world. Like new lovers, content in each other's gaze.

Later while I sat drinking a beer with Una, I told her about what had happened.

"Amazing," she said.

"Amazing," I echoed. "What are the chances she'd remember us? I can't help thinking the meeting wasn't by chance. I know it's silly."

"Like it's a sign from India?"

"Yes."

"Lesley … I think she's telling you it's okay for you to move."

The first thing we sold was the sofa. Burgundy leather, with thick pillows and embellished with copper fittings, it looked like it belonged in Sherlock Holmes's study. Apart from the scratches on one of pillows from our dog, it looked barely used. A friend bought it.

I was happy to see it gone. To me, it reeked of exhaustion, desperation, and fear. Looking at it, I saw India sinking into a *grand mal*, her green eyes wild with horror. I heard her telling me she loved me as the seizure pinned her down, her thin arms and legs stiff, her mouth open wide, her red lips turning grey. The choking sound of her trying to catch her breath.

Beds, chairs, desks, lamps, and tables exited daily. Nonetheless, we were worried. We had determined that we would rent out the house for the foreseeable future but couldn't find tenants. Mark put an ad in the local paper but none of the potential renters were quite right. Some loved it but had no money. Others were unprepared to care for an aging home.

I worried nobody wanted it as they thought India had died there. I started to think of the house as a rock tied around my neck, strangling me with its weight.

Mark made endless financial calculations. We could afford to leave if we didn't rent it out but we'd have to be frugal. The kids' drama classes I'd been offered in Penticton would have to run; if not I might have to go back to waitressing.

"We're not staying here," he reassured me. "I don't want to stay."

The day we held our garage sale, it was supposed to rain so we held it inside. Mark transformed the house into a curio shop, with sections devoted to different themes such as travel, vintage clothing, and glassware. All day long people came and went. Some we knew, others saw the sign at the side of the house, facing the store. Things I thought would sell sat on the shelf, while odd things like my CDs sold quickly. A friend, who bought my collection of small porcelain shoes, told me, "I have a friend who believes objects find their homes."

I didn't mind selling off my belongings. In the past, my house would've made a hoarder blush, but now I longed to live without clutter. I could no longer handle the chaos. I needed space.

It was the same with people. I gravitated towards the generous and the self-aware. In the past, I'd be able to deal with my friends' emotional eccentricities. This wasn't to say I could no longer handle emotions: I was fine with the genuine. But I'd lost patience with people's pettiness and fussing. My grief counsellor told me this would change. I had my doubts.

Around two o'clock, a middle-aged couple (Ed and May, I'll call them) came into the house. They were travelling the area in search of garage sales and rental properties. Ed approached Mark and asked, "What's going on?"

"We're moving out west," Mark said.

"What are you doing with the house? Is it rented?"

"Are you looking? You're welcome to look around."

I didn't notice the couple until later when I saw Mark leading them down to the basement. "This is Ed and May," he said. "They really love the house. The way we loved it when we first saw it."

I immediately responded to the couple's enthusiasm. Ed was big, bald, with a white toothy grin and a firm handshake. May, in contrast, was small-boned and shy. They told us they were waiting to find out if Ed had a job in Ottawa. They'd know in the next few days. At the moment they were living in their cottage, two hours from the city.

"I'll call you as soon as I find out about the job," Ed assured us. "We really want this place."

I didn't take the encounter too much to heart, afraid of being disappointed. But Mark had a feeling about them. He kept repeating, "I sure hope he gets that job. They really loved it here."

At the end of the afternoon, a mother and her teenage daughter walked in. The girl was seventeen with lank brown hair, skinny jeans, and a faded T-shirt. When she spoke it was barely audible. She reminded me of the kind of girl India would've liked. She bought India's two Nintendo DS's for five bucks apiece. Mark wasn't sure why he gave her such a deal. There was just something about her that seemed nice.

As they were leaving, I noticed her mother point out a book about drawing Manga.

"Do you like Manga?" I blurted.

"She loves it," her mother said.

"Come with me," I said, leading her to the stairs. "Wait till you see what I have."

India's room was cluttered with her belongings. Piles lay all over the floor, divided into things we were keeping and things we were giving away. "This was my daughter India's room. She loved all kinds of Manga."

"I'm sorry about your daughter," the mother said. I knew she was from the village and probably knew our story.

"Me too," I said.

I handed the girl a stack of Manga. "Do you read these? India could read one in an hour."

"She devours them," her mother said.

"I wasn't sure what I wanted to do with them. But if you'd like them, I'd sell them to you."

The girl nodded. "I'd like them but I only have ten dollars left."

"I'm only charging ten dollars."

I found a box and the girl filled it with books.

"Thank you," the mother said. "Those will keep her occupied for a long time."

"I'm just happy they've found a home."

Several days later, we joined May and Ed at the house. Earlier in the week he'd called to tell us he'd gotten the job, and they wanted the house.

As Mark wandered around the back lot with Ed, I sat on the front steps with May. She was easy to talk to and I understood she took time to consider what she was saying. We talked about our childhoods. We'd both grown up travelling, going to different schools every few years. She told me she was going to use my studio to paint and do her beadwork. I was pleased by that. When we'd first moved to the house I'd used the room to write. Later, I'd escaped there when I needed to cry. After that, I couldn't work there anymore.

"Mark says you're writing a book. What's it about?"

I hesitated. I was leery of telling strangers about my book. It inevitably made them uncomfortable. I was about to give May my standard generalized response, when something stopped me. It's happened to her, I suddenly thought.

"I'm writing a memoir. About my daughter. She died from a very rare disease. Her name was India. That's why we can't live here anymore. It's a beautiful house but –" I stopped. Maybe I'd said too much. Would she want to live here if she knew? "She didn't die here. If you're worried. She died at a hospice in the city."

"I'm not scared of death."

"Most people are," I said.

"I know death," she whispered. "I lost a son." Her eyes brimmed with tears. I nervously reached over to touch her.

"I'm sorry. Recently?"

"He would've been in his twenties now. You never get over it," May said. "You just sort of learn to live with the pain."

6

Up in Her Room

Dad, my body is a lot like the country of India. Parts of it are at war like India and Pakistan. And it has a lot of earthquakes.

– India Taylor, September 2011

My heart rattled like a heavy key chain whenever I entered it. Once inside, I'd pace back and forth, flop on her bed, bury my nose in the stuffed animals that lay across it. Sometimes I imagined the room still smelled of her. I'd gulp the air, trying to eat it. At other times I'd stand in front of the window, fingering her jewellery, studying her belongings, trying to remember their origins.

People were always giving India things, even before she got sick. She'd go out for lunch with friends and return with a new treasure: a cashmere hat, a new teddy bear, a new hoodie. She might not ever look at this new possession again, but if I recommended donating it to the local thrift shop, she'd look at me as if I'd suggested cutting off her arm. I had to hide any clothes I wanted to get rid of, even if she hadn't worn them in years. I'd wait until she'd left the room before sneaking them into the donations bag.

India was a collector. A mythic magpie of a girl,

stealing shiny objects to line her nest. There was never enough room for her belongings. Instead of one jewellery box, she had three, each crammed with oddities: a grain of rice with her name written on it, a jade wolf charm, a key chain from Paris, a cheap Star of David on a silver chain, the last a souvenir from her mild obsession with her Jewish great-grandmother, of Hungarian descent.

It was an obsession that triggered more collecting: when India was about twelve, she liked to pretend she was Jewish. She'd even tell people she was, though she knew nothing about the religion. That year she read everything she could get her hands on about World War Two: *The Diary of Anne Frank*, *When Hitler Stole The Pink Rabbit*. We'd watch movies like *The Boy in the Striped Pyjamas* and I'd cry. She'd research the historical facts behind the story on the computer, always curious about the places these events happened. Other mothers I knew were aghast that I encouraged this. They thought it was too morbid and would give her nightmares. It never did. Instead it seemed to fuel an ever-increasing interest in the world. One of her prized possessions was a huge world history book that Mark and I gave her for Christmas one year. She'd sit in her bed and look at it when she was too tired to be social.

And then there were the hats. When India was about two we went to see a psychic, who had an office in downtown Ottawa in an old stone United Church. The psychic – known as the Angel Lady – was very popular, with a six-month waiting list. She was so highly regarded that eventually she went to work with the Toronto police. The day of my appointment, I remember her leaning across the table in her little room and asking softly, "Why does your baby have so many hats?" This had made me smile as I was constantly buying India hats. I couldn't stop.

India loved hats. There were piles of them in her room, hanging on her coat rack, downstairs in the closet. Hats of every kind: Manga-inspired hats with devil horns or shaped liked rabbits, peaked caps, woolen toques, fedoras with funky trim, a black broad-brimmed '60s-inspired number I'd bought at H&M but never wore. I took photos of her in this one ... some of the last I ever took. In them, she's lying across the bed, her arms folded across her pillow, her shoulders bare. A lock of her black hair rests on her forehead. With her arched eyebrows and full mouth, she looks like Jean Shrimpton, a model famous in the '60s. One can almost believe she's in David Bailey's studio and there's an adoring makeup artist waiting to powder her face. That day I remember thinking it was a good omen that she wanted her photo taken. I told myself if she had the energy to do this, she must be feeling better. But my daughter was like that. Even when she was feeling terrible she could always summon the energy to do something theatrical.

When she was eight, we visited my parents in Spain for Christmas. I have a photo of our arrival in Alicante. India and I are sitting in the back of my father's compact car. My short hair is dishevelled. I look tired. A scrappy wool scarf is wound about my neck. India is leaning against me, wide awake. She's wearing my navy beret, probably stolen from me. Here, once again, she looks as if she belongs in another era, the '30s. It would be hard to match that '60s girl in the black hat with this creature, an earlier version of her. Here she's Greta Garbo in *Blue Moon,* with her blonde hair, porcelain skin, and wide angular cheekbones.

This is the thing about India: she's hard to pin down. One moment she's an eight-year-old on holiday in Spain, insisting on swimming in the pool despite the fact it's winter. The next she's in a restaurant overlooking the sea, chatting up the waiter and eating a plate of escargot, a sophisticated thirty-year-old world traveller locked in a child's body.

My father even lost a hat to her, a brimmed grey tweed, the kind one imagines a British lord of the manor wearing while walking his Labradors. My mother swiped it off his head and gave it to India. She said it looked better on her. India wore these hats everywhere, even in bed.

In Mark's office, hanging on the wall, is one of India's favourite hats. It's a modern take on a Chairman Mao hat in brown linen. When I look at it, I can picture India sitting next to me in the car, wearing it with her khaki fall coat, trying to find a song she liked on my iPod, or fiddling with the car's controls. (After she died, I had to get used to doing that for myself. I wasn't really sure what all the dials did. It was always she who adjusted them.) Perhaps we're on the way to her singing lesson, or I'm taking her shopping. We don't talk a lot. We don't have to. We know how to be quiet in each other's company. Or maybe she's talking so much I can barely keep up, telling me how she wants to move to Japan when she grows up and work in animation as a voice actor. Perhaps she's talking about all the places she wants to travel to when she grows up: Hungary, Korea, Czechoslovakia, Russia, Germany, Italy.

While I was writing this I had to stop myself from writing *when she died* rather than "grows up." An odd burp in my consciousness? Or perhaps part of me believes that's where she is now. If I'm honest, that's what I imagine when I'm feeling hopeful: that she's hovering over all those places she dreamt of. Swooping down from the air like a pigeon who's spotted a bread crumb in St. Mark's Place, watching the tourists and laughing to herself, *Look at me. I'm so free and you're all so stuck in your bodies.* This is when she isn't busy making out with Cory Monteith, the actor from *Glee*. I imagine that too. This makes me sound crazy, I know. I rarely think of her as dead and gone. How can I? She's so alive in my imagination. Some would probably consider this a trick to soothe my grief. It very well might be. My logical mind understands only too clearly her demise. It recognizes the cruelty of death. It's not that I can't accept this reality. I do. It's just that part of me doesn't believe it's the end.

The walls in India's room were orange and red. She chose the colours herself, her first grown-up room. She said she wanted something fiery and alive. My mother and I helped India with the painting. She painted sitting down. Her hands trembled while she worked but she didn't want to stop. We painted late into the night.

My mother worked long after India and I gave up. She said the colours reminded her of a whorehouse, but she wasn't going to say anything to India. She wanted her to be happy.

I could see my mother's point. The room, with its slanted roof and wainscoting, resembled a set from a TV movie about the Old West. All that was missing was a couple of busty women in corsets. At the side of the room, there was a makeshift closet that resembled a stage, a dressing area of sorts. Later we stuck a red sofa there. The colour clashed with the walls, but India liked it as it made the room feel like an apartment.

The sofa was always covered with piles of her belongings: T-shirts, scarves, odd socks, sketchbooks, half-read novels, unfinished homework, and CDs. India never sat there. She was always in bed. Even when we first moved there. She spent hours in bed drawing and singing, rarely venturing out except for school or to join us downstairs for a movie.

Sometimes her best friend, Ally, would spend the night. She'd sleep on a mattress on the floor next to India's bed. I'd hear them whispering. I'd strain trying to hear what they were talking about but I never could quite make out what they were saying.

A month or so after India died, I found her diary, one my mother had given her when she was ten or eleven. I'd forgotten about it. I never expected her to use it. It's large with a blue patent leather cover and a lock. India had written her name on it. Her writing is pointed and sharp, like the scrawl of the EEG machine that recorded her seizures.

"How can you be a writer? I hate writing," India used to tell me. "I can never think of anything to say."

For a few minutes, I hesitated about opening the diary. It had always been important to me to respect her privacy. Besides, I knew she wouldn't like me snooping. She used to shout at me to leave her alone if she was watching one of her romantic Korean soap operas – I guess having her mother there destroyed the mood. I wasn't sure what I'd find, if anything. To tell the truth, I was afraid there'd be something about me. A badly scribbled line or two calling me mean or a bitch.

Instead I found diary entries written by both Ally and India. A list of the boys they liked, with names like characters from soap operas. I never knew about these dalliances. The boy who held India's hand when they went to the movies for Ally's twelfth birthday. India wrote she was so nervous she didn't know what to do. What if he wanted to kiss her? Reading this, I almost said out loud, *Kiss him back, India, that's what you do – go for it*. Of course, if I'd known about this and said anything, she'd have told me to mind my own business.

There was a paragraph about a boy she liked. I couldn't make out his name but I have my suspicions. If it's who I believe it is, he has the same long lean build as her and the same black hair. He also shared her wry sense of humour and inventiveness. She wrote that she'd been to his house and that it smelled so good because it smelled of him. How odd that she'd been in love and that I'd never known.

There was a boy I knew about. He might've been her first love. She'd met him at an overnight arts summer camp where I had been an instructor. I taught drama but she took art. The boy was in class with her. He was a lovely artist, but such a perfectionist that if his drawing didn't work out, he'd cry with frustration. She was twelve and he was sixteen, although observing them, it would've been easier to believe it was the other way around. Psychologically she was much older than him. He was shy and struggled to look people in the eye when he spoke to them. India talked to everybody. On the camp movie nights, they'd position their pillows next to each other, their feet gently looping around each other's. She was probably his first crush. I think she was his. Every time I looked around he was there with her.

The other instructors thought their friendship was sweet and were always talking about it to me. I don't know why, but it bothered me. He was a nice boy, gently keeping an eye on her. I guess I was jealous. I tried not to let it show, but it did. Not that she even noticed. She was too busy. India was sick then, but still herself, and it never occurred to me that she might die, so it wasn't that. It was more a gnawing reminder that our children abandon us eventually for their own lives. That summer she was coming into her own. So confident, trying every class the camp offered – even drumming, despite the fact that her shaking made it difficult for her to maintain a beat. One night at the camp talent show, she stood up and sang a song by Coldplay. I couldn't watch. I stared at the ground, scared she'd have a seizure. She didn't. Afterwards, the camp cook turned to me and said, "When your daughter sings, it's like she's with God."

India's romance fizzled after the camp. In the months following, her health took a turn for the worse. She spent more and more time in the wheelchair. She was in and out of the hospital, her diagnosis constantly evolving. They did go out on a date the next winter. She was on the MCT diet and doing so well, Mark and I agreed she could spend the afternoon downtown with her friend. We were still worried enough that we stayed downtown so if she needed help we could get to her.

They met at the War Memorial. I remember watching her walk across the pavement to him, scared she would slip on some ice. It was difficult to watch India walk even when she was doing well. She always looked as if she was about to tip over, like a drunk winding his way home.

Mark was just parking the car at the mall when his phone rang. It was a stranger, at the mall, a woman who'd stopped to help India after she'd fallen over. She said India was bleeding badly. When we got there, India was standing next to her friend, her face and hands covered in blood. The woman who'd called was helping her. The boy was standing there, immobile. India couldn't tell us what had happened but it was clear she'd smashed her face against something sharp. I thought she might have broken her nose. It was swollen, twice its usual size. The skin above her lip was scraped and inflamed, her lips puffy. Mark thought she should go to the hospital, but India was adamant that her date continue.

I took her to the bathroom and washed her face gently, afraid of hurting her. Cleaned up, it didn't seem so bad. She looked as if she'd been in a car accident. I told her I thought we should go home but she wouldn't listen. Finally, we reached a compromise. The date would continue. They could visit the art gallery but only if India agreed to be in a wheelchair.

I don't know what Mark and I did with ourselves while they visited the gallery. The hours she was gone must've been insufferable. I have a vague notion that we sat in the car, drank coffee and waited, not saying much, voicing our worries every so often when they became too big to keep in.

India rarely mentioned this boy after her fall, I thought maybe because he didn't call her again, but it was India who'd lost interest. Mark found messages from him to her on her Facebook account that she never answered. I sometimes wonder how he took the news she'd died. His mother sent us a note of condolence so he must have known.

After Mark and I returned from spending the winter at my parents' house in Gibsons, I found one of India's drawing books lying on the sofa in her room. The cover was ripped off and it was stained with coffee. The edges looked as if they'd been chewed by mice. While we'd retreated to the west coast over the winter they'd taken over the empty house, even burrowing into the box I kept India's mittens in. I flipped through page after page of her artwork: drawings of girls in Japanese school uniforms, lovers entwined in each other's arms, drawings of Ally and herself. In the middle of the book, I found some writing. It said, "Nobody loves the sick girl." Immediately I shut the book. I hid it in a drawer in our bedroom. I don't know if I was protecting Mark or myself.

In the last two months of India's life, her bedroom be-came her world. Day after day, she lay in bed. I don't dare let myself consider what she thought or worried about. I'm a coward. When I began my blog about India, I decided not to write about her feelings; that would be an invasion of her privacy. I still believe that. And I know that I don't know how she felt: I've never been sick for more than a week. Most of the time I imagine she was too tired to think about much at all. In a way I'm grateful for this. I could fill my head with what-ifs until it burst: What if she had questions or fears she wanted to share but she sensed I couldn't han-dle them? What if she tried to talk about these things and I wasn't sensitive enough to pick up the clues? What if I failed her?

Writing these words, I have the urge to go into the kitchen and pour myself a tequila. Drink it down, and let it burn my memories away. If only alcohol worked. But I know from experience that this regret can't be sedated. It's a creature that breathes independently. Like the fire-breathing Cherufe of Chilean mythology, it craves sacrifice. What else have I left to give? There's nothing left, only my memories.

For hours, I sat at the end of her bed knitting while she fell in and out of sleep. At other times, I sat in a chair next to her bed and held her hand (I became good at texting with one hand). I cuddled her even when she didn't want me to. If she'd been willing, I'd have lain in her bed and cuddled her all the time, but she got fed up with me and pushed me away. Then, I thought it was because the bed was too small. Now, I wonder if she could feel my fear.

During these days and nights I hated her room. One night, as I lay watching a movie with her, I was struck by the strange contrasts surrounding us. It wasn't the way a teenage girl's room was supposed to be. It looked like it belonged to a woman in her nineties. Not sure how to handle the emotions, I addressed my observations to her. A poem of sorts.

"My sixteen-year-old daughter's room: Fire red walls, a reproduction of a Chagall painting, the one with the bride, and a horse encircled by summer flowers, postcards from Ibiza, Banff, Manchester, Madrid, Tokyo, Halifax, and Paris taped to the wall, a poster of that guy, the one from that British boy band your dad can't stand. Over the window, a dream catcher, over your bed a medicine wheel. A stuffed kangaroo, a crocheted monkey, and a plastic horse covered in green marker. Those earrings with the pink skulls on them. Deodorant that smells of watermelon. A box filled with your drawings. An Indian flag, the old TV, black nail polish, baby blue eye shadow, lipstick the colour of bubble gum. Your iPod, cotton balls, toilet paper, a white basin, Band-Aids, head phones, a sponge, your toothbrush, a commode, a grade ten math book that you never opened. A box of latex gloves, a syringe, bottles of Valproic Acid, Keppra, Clobazam and the dreaded Ativan – I can't look at it without thinking of the time they gave it to you at the hospital and later at home you thought the Spanish lady in the painting in the living room was winking at you – and finally, a hospital bed."

When we moved out of the house, India's was the last room we cleaned out. Neither Mark nor I could face it. Our friends Una and Shauna took turns helping us. Mark and I made stacks of things to keep, things to get rid of. Before anything went into the donation box, we took time to go through each other's choices.

We sat on the floor with Shauna, sorting through India's artwork, marvelling at her productivity. There must've been twenty sketchbooks, as well as piles of drawings. It was impossible to choose between them, so unless they were stained or ripped we kept them. Shauna sorted them into boxes by size. Sometimes one of us would find a particularly good one and show the others. Then we'd all fall silent for a moment, contemplating the same unanswerable question: why?

After India died, I was always careful to close the door whenever I'd visited her room. I thought I could lock the past in there – stop the memories from bleeding into the corridor and down the stairs into the rest of house. As I finish this chapter, I'm aware that I'm doing this again, though only symbolically.

The last time I entered India's room it was empty except for some books waiting to be shipped to the local thrift shop. It looked very small but it still felt dangerous. The feeling reminded me of visiting monuments such as the Black Hole of Calcutta, or the Witch Trials Monument in Salem, Massachusetts. Even though the tragedy is over, I can't help but feel that the place itself remembers, and shudders with grief. To me, India's room is like a cell where I watched her being tortured ... where she was forced to shake hands with her tormentor. What might others see? A pretty room with a view of a small woods and a farmer's field. A place to fall asleep, watching the moon.

7

Stay Gold

I never noticed colors or clouds and stuff until you keep re-minding me about them. It's almost like they weren't there before.

> – S.E. Hinton
> *The Outsiders*

I wake up with a start. India is screaming. Giant cockroach-es are coming to kill her. She's shaking, her eyes round and huge. I don't know what she's talking about. I tell her she's just having a bad dream. She clutches my arm, pulls me tightly. I tell her she's okay, that I would never let anything hurt her. I believe this when I say it, but now, I wonder if she must have thought I was a liar.

She wants me to sleep with her. There's not enough room in her bed, the hospital bed I've come to hate with all my being. The day they delivered it, I ran out of the house screaming, down the winding road, past the red brick church, the yellow house that was once a schoolhouse to-wards the farmhouse on Wood's Road. I would've kept running but a school bus came barrelling by so fast I was almost knocked down. I lost my temper and screamed ob-scenities at the driver. "Fuck you! Why the hell don't you watch where you're going!" The bus driver stopped the bus, opened the door, and screamed back at me. Later I found out she was my new neighbour.

I drag the mattress from Mark's office into India's room. Even as I do this, I worry that I'm taking too long. I sleep on the mattress with my arm held up so I can hold India's hand. Her skin is soft, almost like a baby's. But her colour is changing; there's a tinge of yellow to it that I don't like.

Throughout the night, she wakes me. The cockroaches are coming. "Help me, Mummy, please."

I don't know what to do to reassure her. I'm not thinking straight. For the last year, Mark and I have been taking turns getting up at two a.m. to give her meds. I'm exhausted.

All night long, her sleep is disturbed by these hallucinations. I lose count of them.

I've never known my daughter to be afraid like this. I try everything I know. For a while I sing Rafi songs, the kind she liked when she was a toddler. *Down by the bay where the watermelons grow ...* She joins in, singing a few words and then falling silent as she's pulled under by another seizure.

I tease her, singing loudly. When she was little, she used to press her small hands against my lips and say, "Don't sing, Mummy. Don't sing." But she doesn't react. She's too tired to play the game.

Whenever I think the worst is past she has another hallucination. The insects are crawling up the walls, climbing on the bed, they are coming to kill her. In the midst of the torture, the seizures come, offering her relief from the terror as she sinks into oblivion. This is the only time I've ever been grateful for the seizures. At least when she's having one – which is about every five seconds – she's free of the fear.

In the beginning when India started having the seizures, she would see the worry on my face and say, "Don't worry, Mummy, they don't hurt." I believed she was telling me the truth, though I know she often tried to shield me. Of course, there was pain. She had accidents all the time. Once when we were sitting at my desk, watching a music video on You-Tube, she lost consciousness and her head hit the desk so hard she broke a tooth.

Throughout the last six years, the days have been stained by accidents: a fall at the bowling alley, at someone's birthday party, while dancing, during her piano lesson, getting off the bus from school. Her body was a quilt of bruises. Every day something happened. There were probably accidents she never told me about. But for the most part, there was no fear. India would brush herself off, take a moment to gain her composure, and continue what she'd started.

The only things that scared her before the hallucinations were wolves and *grand mal* seizures. Mark had read her *The Wolves of Willoughby Chase* as a bedtime story when she was about nine and Joan Aiken's vivid descriptions of the wolves' cruelty were etched on her psyche.

I take my daughter's hand and hold it tight. "The insects aren't real, India," I whisper. "It's just your mind playing tricks on you."

My words don't offer any comfort. I teach her relaxation exercises I learned at drama school. I get her to make her body as rigid as possible then relax each limb slowly. India's constant seizing makes this a slow process. Every twenty seconds I have to repeat my instructions. We repeat the procedure over and over for an hour or so. This works for a while. Or at least, it seems to distract her.

I crawl into her bed, nuzzle against her. She's warm and smells of flower-scented shampoo and sweat. I want to wrap myself around her and protect her like I did when she was a baby. At the same time, I'm so tired, I feel as if I'm being pulled away from her and I can't fight it.

Finally, we fall asleep.

Early in the morning, around six, Mark comes to bring her medicine. He takes my place and I go to our bedroom to sleep. When I finally wake up, I can tell by looking at the panic in his green eyes that it's continuing.

Mark and I don't know why this is happening. None of the doctors have ever said a word about hallucinations. Yes, we understand they say she's going to die but we don't think this is connected with that. India's recently been given a steroid infusion at the hospital. It's supposed to buy her time until the scientist working on her cells can come up with something. She's still on a low dose. Our friend Chris hears about what's happening to India and tells us she went psychotic when she was on steroids.

Mark phones India's neurologist, tells him what's happening. He says we should wean her off the steroids. We wait, watching her every gesture. Positive this is just a glitch. Soon India will be back to her usual self, making jokes and demanding Singapore fried noodles and poutine.

People transform in front of India's eyes. While Shauna, her caregiver, feeds her, she says, "You're all yellow," and laughs unsurely.

When I come upstairs to join them, she tells me, "Mummy, you look like a giant pineapple."

I'm relieved that these new hallucinations make her laugh. We can joke about how silly they are. These don't last long, however. Soon the crueller visitations begin to appear during the day.

This goes on for several weeks. It's becoming clear it's not the steroids causing the hallucinations. It's something else.

Twenty-one-year-old Shauna is supposed to be leaving to go on an exchange to New Zealand to work on a sheep farm. She has a sheep farm in the next village from ours and she's keen on learning how they do things overseas. The organization she's going with is having trouble finding her a placement. She's not sure when she's supposed to go, only that it's soon.

She's been with India four years. They share the ultimate girl bond: a passion for horses. India loves Shauna like a sister. It's Shauna who knows how to lift her spirits, bringing tiny Lionhead bunnies for her to play with when she's stuck in bed.

Mark and I trust Shauna as if she were blood. She's strong and smart. Not at all squeamish. She's more than a caregiver: she's family. The three of us depend on her. She knows everything about us. But I want her to go to New Zealand. She deserves an adventure. I know she doesn't want to leave India. She's afraid India will die when she's in New Zealand and she wants to be close when that happens. She makes me promise I'll call her and tell her when it gets to that point. I want to honour her wishes but I'm conflicted. Shauna is young and I don't want her to be burdened with all this sadness. Still, I promise as I know it's what she wants. I tell myself when the times comes I will insist she doesn't travel back.

I don't want to think of my daughter dying but I can think of nothing else. I'm scared. The fear burns through me. It's as if I've ingested burning coals. I imagine everyone can see the heat when I speak. My words are feverish and senseless. I can't keep on focus. Putting the kettle on for tea, I stop midway, kettle in hand as I wonder what I'm supposed to do. My shoulders and back are hard, fortified with tension. I take shots of rye. The alcohol doesn't make me drunk. It just calms me like a shot of morphine. I don't know why this is. Perhaps it's my sympathetic nervous system taking over, the adrenaline rushing through me, the energy I still have despite the exhaustion making it impossible to get drunk. I don't want to get drunk anyway. I know too well that will just make me sadder. I just need to be tranquilized so my hands don't shake. I don't want my daughter to see my fear.

Mark and I hire Yolly, a nurse from the Philippines to replace Shauna. We like her from the start. She has a calming, confident manner. She's worked in a home for the elderly and with people who have seizures. I know India will be interested in her because she comes from another culture.

The local Centre Local de Services Communautaires gives us money to pay for twenty hours of help a week. Mark tries to keep up with his clients but it's difficult. He's sleep deprived and his office is across the narrow hall from India's room. We don't have enough money to pay for all the help we need.

Luckily, Yolly is prepared to cook for us and though we're still cooking for India, Mark and I are surviving on whatever we can rummage. Besides, we're so anxious we forget to eat. When we do eat, it's as if we haven't seen food in weeks.

My friend Anita and my parents arrange with a local caterer to deliver us meals every Monday. The portions are generous and we survive on them for days. Other friends hear what's happening and make us food. Jars of pasta sauces, soups, muffins, bottles of wine begin appearing on our doorstep. One of India's friends and her mom send me home every Saturday evening after work with a full meal. My boss and her partner buy us prepared meals from an Ottawa caterer.

These gifts of food sustained us for many months. When I think of the generosity shown to my family during this time I'm incredibly grateful. I know people didn't know what to say to us back then, but the fact they took the time to feed us demonstrated so perfectly that we were in their thoughts.

A month prior to the arrival of the hallucinations, Mark started a campaign to bring awareness to our situation. He created a website called *One Strong Girl* in order to fund the scientist and her lab staff who were trying to find a treatment for India. They were consulting with scientists all over the world, hoping to learn something that might slow the progression of the disease.

Even though I know what Mark is doing is the right thing, by drawing attention to India's plight, I'm scared. It's weird – I feel almost superstitious about it. As if I believe by announcing to the world that she is getting worse it will make her die sooner. It's not logical, but the feeling is ever present. I resent him for fighting too. This, I understand, is because at some deep level I've accepted she will die and I'm petrified that if I allow myself to believe that the researchers can save her and I'm disappointed, I will have to relive the struggle to accept the facts again.

In my heart I want to believe they can fix her. I'm desperate for a made-for-TV ending to our story. But when he tells me about the work the lab is doing, I want to scream at him, *Why are you torturing me?*

Living on the brink of hope and despair is like being part of a trapeze act, constantly somersaulting through space and time, and wondering, no matter how skilled your partner is, if they will be ready to catch you.

Admittedly even as I write that I'd accepted India's certain death, I know this is not a hundred percent correct. I continually normalized every change in India's health. When she stopped being able to feed herself, I found reasons why it was just a temporary problem. When she stopped being able to walk, I researched for hours the side effects of her drugs until I found one of them could cause ataxia.

Mark starts a Facebook page so that people can stay informed. Every day we receive donations and well wishes from strangers, acquaintances, and friends. In Wakefield, our friends Una and Chris, with the help of many generous volunteers, host a fundraiser at Una's café, Le Hibou. Local artists, musicians, and actors donate their time and talent.

The local media hears what's happening and we're visited by interviewers from the *Ottawa Citizen* and the CBC. *The Globe and Mail*'s medical reporter writes an article about the work the lab is doing. As a result the lab receives threats and calls from people begging for their help, people outraged that they aren't trying to help them. It interferes with the running of the lab and causes fear amongst the staff, so we're asked gently not to mention them by name.

What the public doesn't realize is that the lab has been researching the enzyme India's missing for a very long time. And though they are keen to help India, they're hoping to learn from her cells too. They think her cells might reveal clues that will help those suffering from related diseases such as Parkinson's and Alzheimer's as well as children suffering from Spinal Muscular Atrophy (SMA), one of the diseases India has inherited the mutated gene for.

At the fundraiser I meet people I haven't seen in years. Friends come from Ottawa and further away. They bid on the donated artwork and the gifts given by local businesses. It's an odd feeling being the recipient of all this generosity. I would prefer that I was just an ordinary guest. I wish India could be at the benefit, see how much people love her and want her to be healthy again.

In the middle of the evening, I'm approached by the mother of one of my former students. I don't know her particularly well, nor am I close with her child. She tells me her daughter is there and she wants me to see her. I try to make excuses but she's insistent. I don't know how to tell her it causes me pain to see other people's children, especially little girls. The woman is adamant. I can't understand why she's not getting the message. I let her drag me over to her daughter, out of the main room and into the corridor. We are surrounded by people viewing the art hanging there, trying to decide what they want to bid on. I look around, hoping a close friend will pass by, someone who can run interference. There's nobody.

My former student is a pretty girl of ten or eleven. I don't know what to say to her. Usually I'm good with kids but I lack the capacity now. I'm filled with anger. It's not rational, but I don't understand why this woman can't see how forcing me to spend time with her child is cruel.

For about five minutes I make awkward conversation then, finally, I excuse myself. It's not the girl's fault she's healthy. It's not that I wish her otherwise – it's just jealousy.

Throughout the night, people introduce themselves to me. Parents of India's friends I haven't met share stories with me. A woman I don't know but who follows my blog introduces herself. She's in her forties, dark-haired, with caring eyes, the sort of person I imagine might be fun to have a night out with. She tells me reading my blog has changed the way she relates to her teenage daughter. That she used to always argue with her. But since learning about India she's been trying to be gentler, trying to be more understanding. This makes me feel good. She tells me if I ever need anything, I'm only to ask her.

At the end of the evening, I ask to say a few words to the crowd. I get up on the stage and thank them on my family's behalf. I'm told by a friend that I speak eloquently and sincerely. I have no memory of what I said.

The organizers have made a huge card for India. Everybody from the benefit has signed it. When I get home, India is still awake so I show it to her, pointing out her friends' names and her teacher's name. This pleases her. She smiles. I tell her all the lovely things people have said to me about her, how everybody is rooting for her and how they've raised money to help her get well.

Shauna's placement gets delayed further so we keep both caregivers on. At least now with the donation money we don't have to worry about rustling up the cash. One worry is alleviated.

Days and nights merge. I can't tell where one day starts and the other ends. Mark calls the neurologist again; this time he prescribes an anti-psychotic and a sleep aid. The neurologist offers no reason why this is happening or the cause.

I wait with India after she takes the first dose, anxious to see some improvement.

Yolly sees me growing hopeful and, perhaps to save me further pain, says, "Those pills won't work. She's not psychotic."

I know immediately she's telling the truth.

Over the course of India's illness, I've spent hours on the Internet researching progressive epilepsies, even though she tested negative for all of them. (Sadly, I thought this ensured that her disease wasn't fatal.) I was terrified of one disease in particular, Lafora. The geneticist at CHEO must've been worried about this as well because she tested her twice for it.

Lafora is a cruel form of epilepsy that begins in adolescence. Until then, the children, like India, appear healthy in every respect. In fact, also like India, they are often high achievers, doing well in both school and sports. It affects boys and girls equally and is a death sentence. The children usually die in their late teens or early twenties. By then, they are usually unable to do anything for themselves and are tormented by constant seizures and jerks.

Most cases start at about fourteen, when the victim has a *grand mal*. This sets in motion a spiral of symptoms that include unexplained diminishing academic performance, flickering light-induced absence and myoclonic seizures, reports of temporary blindness, visual hallucinations, depression, ataxia, and dementia.

The chances of contracting this illness are about one in a million. Greater odds than India's disease but still rare enough that most people wouldn't give it a second thought.

The family of a young woman with the disease had begun a fundraising site called *Chelsea's Hope*. As India's hallucinations progressed, I read that website repeatedly, trying to understand what was happening to my daughter. As she was the only reported case of her disease, I had nowhere else to look for answers, no mothers to talk to, no inkling of what would come next.

The similarities between the two diseases staggered me. The two symptoms that scared me most were the hallucinations and the dementia. Parents of these children spoke of buying their teenage daughters dolls for Christmas. I started to worry that India's next symptom would be dementia.

The four of us take shifts, sitting in the orange chair in India's room, hunched over her, holding her hand. Most of the time she can't watch TV because the images on the screen are distorted. She won't listen to music. So we talk. Or try to anyway – between the hallucinations and seizures, there is only time for snippets of conversation. Yolly and I chat about her upcoming wedding, her children back in the Philippines. Occasionally India has the strength to join in. Mostly she just listens, holding my hand or curled into the side of me.

Sometimes, hoping to distract her from the hallucinations, I rely on the dogs. I try to teach her dog, Dimitri, a highly-strung spaniel-border collie, tricks. When that doesn't work, I get him to jump up and down from the bed. He's overweight and less agile than our other dog, Finn, an elderly Jack Russell-dachshund, mix so this makes India laugh. Often I get Finn to do tricks like play dead and beg. Though India's the one who taught Finn his repertoire, it seems to entertain her. Dimitri, despite his skittish nature, rarely leaves her side. He lies with her all day and night, being petted. Even when she's in the grip of a seizure he stays waiting for her. If she's scared, she holds on to him. I tell her, "He won't let anything happen to you." Even as I say it, I know I'm a fraud. Dimitri loves her so much that if he accidentally gets locked out of the room, he whines until we let him back in.

Mark and I try to sleep when we have helpers. Often I cry myself to sleep or lie there trying to make sense of what's happening. Or we sit outside on the front porch theorizing about what's happening to our daughter. He's more hopeful than I. He believes in the power of science.

Plus he's working furiously to get India the chance to try a new medical cannabis called Charlotte's Web created by the Stanley Brothers in Colorado to control seizures. The Stanley Brothers have contacted him and want to donate a treatment. They've heard about India through the media and though nobody feels it will cure her, they believe it might offer her some relief from the relentless seizures and hallucinations. Mark and I are both eager. It's our opinion that it can't be any more damaging than the traditional drugs, and we're running out of options. Our application to the Special Access Program has been denied.

This is a Canadian government program that allows people with terminal illnesses the opportunity to try medicines that have yet to be approved. A sort of last case scenario thing. Our doctors all supported our application so we can't figure out why we weren't approved. Undeterred, Mark has teamed up with a lobbyist he knows and is trying to get in to see the health minister so he can plead our case. We've been warned by the lobbyist not to talk about it. The current Conservative government doesn't react kindly to being pushed, so it's important that when we do share our story with the media that it's planned out carefully. So we wait, planning and strategizing.

We aren't sure what to do. We wonder if maybe we should just drive to Colorado and take up residency. But we worry she won't survive the trip. And what if she needed medical attention? There'd be no coverage. We even consider smuggling it into Canada but this idea is not realistic, and could hurt the Stanley Brothers.

To this day, I don't know if the treatment would've offered her any relief, but it saddens me that perhaps there was the tiniest of chances it might have.

One day as I'm talking to Shauna in the kitchen she starts to cry. Like us, she can't stand to see India tortured. "I'm sorry, I'm so sorry," she says. She doesn't need to apologize. We're all unravelling. Besides, her tears are only proof of how much she adores India.

I start smoking again. I sit hunched up on the porch, and beg God continually to cure India. I go on drives to the supermarket and screech at God. Plead with God. I tell God, I will do anything for him if he'll just fix her.

On my way to work I listen to music, and sing at the top of my lungs like India once did. Driving home, as soon as I head up the hill from Alcove towards Lascelles, my body starts to hurt. A tightness builds in my chest as though someone has a hold on my neck and is squeezing the breath out of me. Hope is difficult to sustain. It takes a physical toll on a person. It's as if before I reach the final stretch to our house I can pretend that my little girl is going to get better, but once I'm on that last approach I know it's useless.

The stress is taking a toll on me. I'm no longer the person I was when India first got ill. Never again will I experience the feelings of invincibility I once enjoyed. When I'm with India, I do my best to hide my fear, but more and more I'm relying on my talents as an actress. I'm determined to protect her, keep her safe from my fears. But the veneer is cracking. Life is teaching me that bad things don't just happen to other people. But it's my goal, no matter what arises, to keep an open vulnerable heart. Not for myself, but for my daughter.

Yet one night driving home from work, I listened to a documentary on the CBC about a woman fighting for the rights of female inmates to keep their babies with them in prison. I don't know how long she'd been in prison; my impression was that it had been years. The interview takes place in the woman's kitchen while she's making cookies with her daughter. In the background her little girl is chattering non-stop as the interviewer asks the mother questions. I can tell from the little girl's singsong voice that she's around three and that she adores her mother, a feeling that's clearly recip-rocated. It reminds me of watching India make piecrust with my mother at the same age and the pleasure she seemed to get from learning something new. It makes me wish I'd taken more time to savour that moment.

The interviewee is an articulate woman, and I'm moved by the sincerity with which she expresses her plight and those struggling in similar situations. But suddenly without any warning I'm filled with rage and begin shouting at the radio, "I've never done anything wrong! Why should I lose my child but you get to keep yours?" I pound my hands on the steering wheel, press my foot down on the accelerator.

Looking back, I now understand what angered me about the interviewee was that I sensed she felt victimized and in my irrational state I was unable to empathize with the circumstances of her life that had led her towards the choices she'd made. In other words, I hadn't considered what writers call her back-story. Instead everything seemed black and white. She'd made a mistake; she deserved to be pun-ished. I, on the other hand, was innocent of any wrongdoing and therefore a real victim. When my outburst was over, I felt ashamed.

As a feminist and a mother, obviously I'm deeply con-cerned with the rights of all parents and believe strongly that as a society we should support those who are struggling. But I'd allowed myself to be engulfed in hatred and jealousy. Immediately I understood this is how people become bitter.

All day long at the knitting shop women come in with their children. I watch them, filled with envy. I want to do things with my daughter. I want her to do what she loves. A woman comes in to take a private class and my col-league teaches her how to knit. From the front of the store,

I can hear her complaining about the way her twenty-year-old daughter dresses, the subjects she's studying in school, and how fed up she is with her, and how she thinks she'll be supporting her forever. Rage fills me. I turn the music up in the store, try to ignore this woman, fight the urge to grab her by the scruff of the neck and tell her how bloody lucky she is. I wouldn't give a damn what India would do as long as she was well again.

As Yolly predicted, the anti-psychotics are useless. The hallucinations become more and more pervasive. Anything India looks at is transformed into something villainous and cruel.

The nights are the worst, but even during the day when she naps she often wakes up sobbing. Sometimes when I'm lying chatting with her, she'll suddenly say, "Mummy, over there, look over there, Mummy. It's coming for me." I hug her to me as close as I can and shout at the nightmare.

As I can't convince her that these horrors don't exist, I've begun fighting them. I shout at them, "Go away!" or "Fuck off!" I've become a warrior in her battle, engaged with the unseen. I tell India to yell too.

"Go away!" she screams. "Leave me alone!"

She never swears, even though I told her when she turned sixteen she was allowed to.

If Yolly or Shauna are with us, they join in. I love Yolly for how she defends my daughter. If I were a hallucination and Yolly yelled at me, I would never come back.

Our household is at war with death. None of us are willing to give India up.

My new tactic of dealing with the hallucinations by engaging with them is working better than when I tried to convince her they weren't real. So I begin to arm her with a host of magical implements. The first of these is a wand. I find the sceptre we gave her on her sixteenth birthday. I tell her it will give her magic and protect her. I'm not sure why she accepts this. When she was a toddler and I'd call her doll a baby, she'd correct me instantly and say, "Mummy, it's a doll." As if she really felt sorry for me believing it was a real baby. Maybe by this point, reality has been so transformed by the hallucinations she believes anything is possible.

I explain that when the cockroaches come, she's to wave her wand and say, "Abracadabra, cockroaches be gone."

We repeat the words together.

The wand gives her strength. It doesn't stop the hallucinations from attacking, but it gives her some psychological power. She's ferocious, arguing loudly with the attacking creatures, and waving the wand. The problem is that each time she seizes, the wand falls from her grasp. Several times she comes close to poking herself in the eye. Next, I try a magic cloak. That doesn't work as well. She needs something that helps her fight back.

I find two silver charm bracelets my mother bought for India and me in Spain. The bracelets are bright and pretty. When shaken they make a sound that reminds me of the noise a fairy's wand might make. I put one on India, the other on myself.

"This is a magic bracelet," I tell her. "It will protect you."

Now when the cockroaches appear we move our wrists and jangle the bracelets as we scream at them to go away.

She likes this. Sometimes when I sleep with her at night, I can hear the sound of her moving the bracelet.

Sundays are the hardest days for Mark and me. Both caregivers are usually off. Sometimes Shauna comes to give us a few hours break so we can eat or, in theory, nap. Mark and I take short turns sitting with India. This is because being with her is so emotionally wrenching that we need an hour or two afterwards to brace ourselves.

Mark says. "It's like watching your child tortured in front of you, over and over again."

I begin reading blogs about grief and loss, trying to understand what it will feel like. Grieving begins a long time before the person actually dies. There's a grief inherent in having to imagine the death of your child. It's as if the world becomes both heavy and light at the same time. The knowledge pushes down on you as if it's an object and its mass has increased a hundred times. The lightness comes from the fact that there's no longer anything to lose.

In hindsight, I understand, I'd begun grieving the moment India got ill. From the start, I was the witness to all her daily losses. Over the years, of course, these grew into bigger losses: losing the ability to draw, play soccer, sing. She rarely spoke of what this meant to her. Perhaps, like me, she tried to view her state as temporary. Soon she would get better.

When she'd ask me, "What happened, Mummy? I used to be normal," I can't remember what I said. Probably that the doctors were working to make her well or that I'd never give up until she was well again. (I wish I had a better answer.) Maybe I said if I could take her place I would. I hope she knew I meant that.

For myself, it seemed as if one day I was a young mum, celebrating my daughter reaching milestones like learning to walk and then suddenly fifteen years later I was supporting her as she tried to walk a few feet across the room. I only ever imagined these things happened in fairy tales or movies. Even then, there'd always be a happy ending.

Before I had India, I was happy about things which seem so transient now. A new pair of shoes, a raise at work, losing weight. I loved Mark, but even that in retrospect to a degree was self-serving. It felt good to be with him. I liked that he loved me. It served me to love him. The return was immense.

But it was different with India. As soon as I first held her, squeezed her small body against me, I was irrevocably changed. My happiness became perpetually associated with hers. (As I write this, all I can think of, as sentimental as it sounds, is the idea that our souls linked arms.)

When India rode her bike for the first time and laughed, this was my joy. At eight, when she got lost and cried in the Indian restaurant because she insisted on going to the bathroom by herself, I felt her panic. This may seem a simple sentiment. But the point is after inhabiting my child's joy so completely, how could I contemplate her death? And if I survived, what could possibly make me whole again?

The tone of the conversations Mark and I have on the porch start to go in a new direction. We talk less of a possible cure or treatment and more of the reality of India's impending death. To say we hoped for her death would be wrong. Neither of us wanted her to leave us, but watching your child suffer is like being repeatedly given electric shocks. It leaves you stinging and dazed.

At this time, a close friend of ours suggested we visit the local shaman. I'll call him J for the sake of his privacy. She'd told him about India and he wanted to help.

This might seem like an odd thing to do when your child is dying, but by this time we were receiving very little guidance from the traditional healers and we were willing to do anything. We never heard from the doctors unless we called them. Our friend Janet, the United Church minister, frequently visited us. She was supportive and wise. Her visits helped both Mark and me because she'd experienced a great deal of grief herself so she understood or at least was unafraid to empathize with our pain.

I'd always been open to all sorts of philosophies on the idea of God. My own concept of God is a mixture of the best of Buddhism, Wiccan, Hinduism, and Christianity. Not very concrete, I'm afraid. I'm not a Christian but I know my Bible; as a teenager, I'd been to a Christian boarding school, but I couldn't tolerate the prejudice and the pettiness I found within its confines. In short, I consider myself open to all sorts of ideas.

Mark, on the other hand, is an adamant and vocal atheist. But he agreed to see J.

Before we went I talked to friends who'd seen J. They all recommended him, even if they couldn't clearly explain what he'd done for them. Everyone seemed to unanimously agree he was a gentle soul.

His house was in the village next to ours. It was surrounded by forest and womb-like circular gardens and small stone walls. Tibetan prayer flags hung on trees and moved listlessly in the September breeze. Over the garage, a Mongolian crest was painted with symbols representing the sky and earth. Strips of material or animal skins hung in some trees. A stone walkway led us to the front door.

J was younger than I expected and slighter. He welcomed us and took us into the living room. A large felted rug decorated with a Mongolian knot dominated the space as well as a tall fig tree. He offered us seats by the fireplace and made us tea. It was green and smelled of the woods. His manner was gentle. I felt I could trust him with a secret. It was difficult to guess his age and there was something priest-like in his manner that made it seem disrespectful to ask. He told us he'd been studying shamanism in Mongolia. He'd been there many times. I remember asking a lot about the country and telling him India was attracted to Asia.

After a while he said, "I'm hoping I'll be able to help you. Can you tell me about India?"

Mark described her illness and the hallucinations. J listened intently, occasionally asking him questions. He told us in his spiritual practice they believed they could contact people's Essential Selves. This struck a chord with me as I believe this core part of our being never dies. He said usually the person was present in these ceremonies but in the past he'd made contact with a person in a coma, and with an infant. He said he done this for people who weren't in the process of dying, but who were struggling. He didn't know where India was in terms of her life journey, but he was willing to try to contact her soul. The only hindrance he could foresee was that her soul would need to give him permission to enter.

Mark and I were both sure she would talk to him. India was such a curious person and I knew she'd respond to his tenderness.

Then J asked me what I wanted him to tell her.

"I'm worried she's hanging on because of us. Tell her she doesn't have to, that we want her to be free." Saying this made me cry. I had to push myself to get the words out. "I don't want her to think I want her to die, I don't. But I don't want her to suffer anymore."

J then asked Mark what he wanted. He said, "Exactly what Lesley said. I want her to be free."

J said he had to go away for a couple of days, but he would call us once he'd held the ceremony.

In the car driving home, both Mark and I both remarked on how we felt better. It was like we'd visited a good therapist and it didn't really matter if what J believed was real or not. Just saying what we wanted for India had given us both a sense of ease.

While J was performing the ceremony for India, I was stuck in rush-hour traffic In Ottawa. Years ago, when India was a baby, a respected psychic who worked for the Toronto police told me India was a mammoth. For years, I'd wondered what she'd meant. At one point when India had worn her hair in long dreads I'd thought this was what she'd referred to. But when I looked up at the car stopped in front of me in the traffic, the first thing I noticed was a sticker of a mammoth on its bumper.

Immediately I knew J had made contacted with India.

I switched my car stereo on and the sound of John Cale's voice filled the car. It was India's song, "Hallelujah" by Leonard Cohen. She used to sing it all the time before the seizures made it impossible to sing. I looked at the clock. It was five-twenty.

That night, Mark and I talked to J on the phone and he confirmed my suspicion that he'd talked to India at that time.

He describes her spirit as that of a blue Mongolian sky horse.

"She's very uncomfortable in her body. It's not a nice place," he says. "I can't find the words to describe it. But what first comes to mind is burned fuses. I don't know if it's her time, but I gave her your message."

The hallucinations get worse. Mark and I have to clear out her room. To India, nothing looks like it's supposed to anymore. We take down her poster from *Totoro*, one of her favourite Miyazaki movies, as well as large Manga posters, as they have started to terrify her. We replace them with a poster of puppies, hoping these will comfort her. Eventually we are forced to take this down too.

We remove photographs, posters of bands, her collection of postcards from around the world. Mark covers the antique light fixture over her bed with her old flannel receiving blankets. For her, the fixture looks like a giant cockroach scurrying across the ceiling.

For a long time, she keeps her beloved stuffed kangaroo and monkey with her. Finally, even these lose their power to comfort her and we take them away. In the end, all that is left are thumbtacks. In due course, these are removed as well. Even the tiniest detail is distorted into the malevolent.

Her room gets stranger-looking each day. As if we're removing her presence, one belonging at a time. In her place, an old, frail, dying woman. Her jewellery boxes and bottles of nail polish have been switched with medicines, washcloths, rubber gloves, tissues, swabs. My daughter is slowly disappearing.

The red walls of her room – she chose the colour herself – overwhelm her so we hang sky blue plastic tablecloths around her bed to hide them. India likes this better and I can't help thinking of the big blue Mongolian sky that J told me is deeply revered in his practice. Maybe, I tell myself, she's preparing to go there. I think about the *Tibetan Book of the Dead*, the idea of Bardo, of rebirth and karmically induced hallucinations. I'd once seen a play based on the book. The idea of it had followed me for days.

Days pass. I sit on India's bed and read to her from an illustrated version of C.S. Lewis's *The Chronicles of Narnia*. I don't know if it will work but I'm hoping to comfort and distract her from the hallucinations. Tonight, though, she's oddly calm and eager to hear the story. We are cuddled together, holding hands. It feels good like in the old days. India is her usual self, scolding me when I skip sections of the story. Her dog, Dimitri, is curled at the end of her bed, and when I lean close to her, I can smell her skin. It smells of freshly baked bread.

When I finish the book, India turns to me and says, "Mum, did you read *The Outsiders*?"

I nod. It had been a long time since we'd talked about books. In the past, it was one of our favourite topics. We both loved to analyze characters and figure out what motivated them.

"Do you remember the end?" She grips my hand tightly.

"I don't. I was in high school when I read that book."

"Remember? Johnny tells Ponyboy to *stay gold*. What do you think that means, Mum?"

"I guess it means lots of things. But mostly I think it means to stay true to yourself no matter what. You know, to stay pure."

India tilts her head and points at me. "Stay gold, Mum."

Afterwards, in bed, I feel optimistic, as if maybe things are going to be okay. For the first time since the hallucinations started I believe we can conquer them.

I tell myself I will read to her again tomorrow. I begin making lists in my head of the books I'll get to read her.

But I never get to. After that night, the hallucinations completely take over her life and my daughter is stolen away from me.

8

So Eden Sank

So Eden sank to grief,
So dawn goes down to day.
Nothing gold can stay.

– Robert Frost
"Nothing Gold Can Stay"

India can't swallow. This means she can't take her medicine.
Mark crushes the pills and mixes them into chocolate pudding. He carefully gives her small spoonfuls. The pudding remains in her mouth. She's thirsty but she can't drink. Yolly takes a syringe and drops water into her mouth. This offers her some relief but not enough to quench her thirst. Mark says, "We have to go to CHEO."

Yolly packs India's belongings, while I scurry around the house trying to find what I will need at the hospital. I'm an expert at preparing for long stays in the hospital. The dogs, sensing something is up, follow me around the house, getting under my feet. I tell myself she can't swallow bxzecause she has a cold. I don't understand what it means when a person loses this ability.

I watch as Yolly dresses India. Stand there, useless and staring. I'm in shock. I tell India we are going to the hospital. She moans, "No, I don't want to."

"We have to," I explain. "You need your meds."

As Yolly is pulling India up from the bed, Dimitri jumps up and pees in a perfect circle around her. I don't think of it at the time; instead all I can think is that we will have to clean the bed, but later I will wonder if he knows what is happening. Maybe he's peed around her to try to protect her, as if he's warning the world she's mine. After all, this creature spent hours lying in her arms. Whoever heard of a spaniel-border collie mix able to stay still so long?

We decide to take two cars to the hospital. Mark and Yolly and India go in his car. I follow them in mine. We meet in the Emergency waiting room. It's crowded, filled with kids with regular ailments: bad coughs, nausea, fevers, and broken limbs. The perils of childhood. I envy their parents. Nobody looks at us. They're all too caught up in their own worry. But I sense they don't want to get too close to us either. India is in and out of consciousness, seizing constantly.

Finally, her name is called by the admissions' nurse. Mark pushes her wheelchair up to the station. The nurse glances at her. I think I see a look of empathy, but I'm not sure. She asks us for India's medical history. I can't believe after all the years we've been coming here that the hospital makes us repeat this every visit. I tell the story, my voice etched with bitterness. I'm rude and I know it. The nurse says, "My daughter has something like this." I stop myself from saying, Yeah, really? Is your child going to die? I'm glad I don't because twenty seconds later, after studying India, she says, "Well, not exactly like this. Not as bad."

This nurse probably won't be able to shake off the worry that will gather inside her from seeing my daughter. I don't want my girl to be a symbol of fear. But I believe when this nurse finally rests her head on the pillow and tries to go to sleep, she will thank God that my daughter is not hers.

The nurse asks for India's Quebec health card and I pass it to her. She studies the photo of a healthy, smiling India and says, "Well, you've all been through quite a journey since that was taken."

I don't know what to say, so I just nod. But once more I feel the tight thread of anger tightening around my throat.

We finish with the formalities and we are led to the nurse's station. The nurse there wants to weigh India. I explain India can't stand but she insists. Surely her dad can hold her up. Anger is building inside me. I can't keep it in. I start to shout, but Mark pushes me gently from the room. I overhear him say to the nurse, "Can't you see we're going to palliative care? What does it matter?"

Finally, we are put in an assessment room. India immediately falls asleep on the bed. She's very peaceful except for the thirst. Yolly asks the nurse for some hydration lollypops. This helps. Yolly is very quiet – she probably understands more about what is happening than Mark and I. She sits next to India and holds her hand. Hours pass. Yolly is due to finish work at five. She tells us to use her while we can, encouraging us to go on little walks. Mark and I take turns going to the cafeteria for coffee. We wait for the doctor for hours. Yolly surprises me, saying angrily, "This would never happen in the Philippines. They would never make such a sick child wait like this."

The on-call doctor finally appears. He orders tests to rule out infections that might explain why India can't swallow. I have no clue yet that time is running out for my daughter. My body is surviving on adrenaline, the way it did in my twenties when I went out dancing all night and had to work the early brunch shift at the restaurant. Nothing makes sense. Time keeps leaping forward then spiralling back. It's like pulling on one of those Slinky toys I was so fond of as a kid.

India's neurologist visits. He stands next to India, holds her hand. He looks sad.

Afterwards the three of us stand in the hallway, as he fumbles with explanations, trying, I think, to tell Mark and me that she's dying. He tells us, "I've seen the way the researchers work. Sometimes things work in the lab but they rarely work on patients." Nurses, patients, and parents brush past us. He never says outright that he thinks she's dying. We've known this doctor three years and I like him. I don't know then that I won't see him again.

The palliative doctor from Roger's House, Dr. M, arrives. She looks young enough to be a high school student. Small-boned and conservatively dressed. She leads us to a private lounge. The kind of room I know from experience that parents are led to when the news is bad. There's a small red sofa and a chair. She sits on the chair. I take a seat next to Mark on the sofa. We look like kids who've been called into the principal's office.

"Not being able to swallow is a sign the body is shutting down," Dr. M says. "India could have a GI tube put in her stomach, but that depends on if a surgeon will do it. She might not be well enough for surgery."

I think about what the doctor has said. I don't completely understand how a surgeon could refuse to do the procedure. I'm trying to get my head around the fact surgery might kill her. "Will that save her life? If we get a GI tube?"

"No, it will just prolong it. It won't stop her dying."

"Would she ever be able to eat again? She loves to eat," Mark says.

"No – Look," Dr. M says softly. "If she goes on the hospital ward, it will be loud. The noise might make the hallucinations worse."

"I don't want her to be afraid," I say. "I don't want that."

Dr. M continues, "If she starts to die here, the staff will have to keep her alive. But if you come over to the hospice, we will make her comfortable. It will be quiet. But don't worry – if you change your minds you can come back here. We won't stop you."

"So if she gets better …" I'm afraid I'm condemning my daughter to death if we go to the hospice.

"I promise you can come back here at any time."

She smiles sympathetically at us. I wonder how many times she's had to do this before. Break parents' hearts.

"Let me give you some time to think. When you decide, get the nurse to call me," she says.

We don't take long to decide. Neither of us can bear the idea of India being further tortured. India is wheeled by the porter from the hospital to the hospice across the street. I'm not sure if she even notices. We are led to our room by Nancy, the admission coordinator.

It looks like a small apartment. In the living area, there's a TV, small fridge, microwave, a comfortable sofa, and a dining table and chairs. In the bedroom we find a regular hospital bed that's been augmented to look as if it's just a funky IKEA-style bed. There are rails on the side but they've been designed to look as if they are stylistic elements. Next to it is a king-size bed. The beds are covered in bright homemade pillowcases and quilts that look as if they've been made by somebody's grandmother. There's no hospital bedding here.

India is moved onto the large bed. All of a sudden, she's screaming again. The hallucinations are back. Mark and I sit by her head, stroking her, telling her she's safe, while our new nurse, Meghan, and Nancy caress her legs. Dr. M watches, studying what's going on. India screams and screams.

"Fuck off," I say to the hallucinations. "Tell them to fuck off, India."

Even now, India is shy about swearing in front of

adults. I tell her again, "It's okay, Indy, tell them to fuck off. You're allowed."

"Fuck off," she says vehemently.

To my surprise, both nurses congratulate her on doing this. This wins my gratitude and my confidence.

She's being tortured again – I can see it in the way she twitches. She looks at me pleadingly. I know she's thinking, Why can't you make them go away, Mummy? I whisper in her ear, "Mummy loves you. Mummy loves you so much." We are back on the battlefield again, throwing insults at the enemy. She raises her wrists to shake her magic bracelet, to rattle it. Her arm falls to the bed. She tries again and the same thing happens.

India turns to Mark. "It's never going to stop."

Dr. M is telling Mark and me about the drugs she's going to try. Their names sound foreign and dangerous. Truth be told, I'm filled with suspicion. Over the last six years I've lost my faith in chemistry. There've been so many medications and none of them ever work. The other truth is, I distrust doctors too. They are not the infallible beings I once believed them to be.

Dr. M decides on three drugs, a powerful anti-seizure med, an anti-psychotic, and morphine. She explains that here at the hospice the emphasis is keeping patients out of pain, rather than worrying about skimping on doses.

I watch nurse Meghan administer the drugs. India doesn't even wince as the needle pierces her skin; she's far-away battling the hallucinations. The drugs take a few minutes to take effect. In the meantime, Mark and I and the two nurses do our best to keep her calm, shouting back at the hallucinations.

Soon she falls into a deep sleep.

I can see by the look on Dr. M's face she's puzzling over India's condition. She says, "Tomorrow I'll ask my colleagues for advice about the hallucinations. Until then, Meghan will keep her sedated and resting."

"Yeah," Meghan says, "I'll be coming in through the night but I'll try not to wake you."

I smile. This means we get to sleep with India. Here in the hospice she won't be hooked up to wires monitoring her heart rate or giving her drugs. Meds will be delivered by injection and she'll be kept hydrated with a bolus. The nurse will listen to her heart and take her pulse.

Lying there, finally, India looks perfectly healthy, an ordinary teenage girl dreaming of her boyfriend. In fact, she looks better than she has for years. Since ending the MCT oil diet a year ago, she's filled out. Her body is curvy and well proportioned. It's hard to connect this image of her to that girl who only a short time ago was screaming. Harder still to imagine is the reality of the illness slowly disconnecting her nervous system from her brain. Her cells are no longer able to clean themselves. The reality of what is going on in India's body is impossible for me to process. I survive each moment by trying to understand what it demands of me.

Meghan asks us if we're hungry and goes off to find us food. It's quiet here, like being in a summer holiday apartment filled with pensioners. The hallways are dark except for the area near the nurse's station. Not far from the station there's a crib. I don't dare look at the sleeping baby. I can tell by its size he or she is struggling.

It's Thursday, a week before Thanksgiving, so the hallways are decorated with pictures of horns of plenty, turkeys, autumn leaves, and Pilgrims. Some of the rooms are empty. There are only a few kids here for respite care. On the doors are name tags, some surrounded by illustrations of flowers, or cartoon characters, or toys.

Meghan brings us a pot of tea and cheese sandwiches. She looks at us as if she's longing to help us, eager to ease our pain. I like her. The way she looks at me reminds me of my friend Una. There's an openness about her. She knows we are in hell. She doesn't try to speak in platitudes or pretend to understand. She just listens as we tell her about our daughter. As we sit here, we are missing another benefit in India's honour. This time her friend Augusta's parents are giving it at their gallery. I feel guilty for not being there, but I understand there's no power on earth that could drag me away from my child. I'm not really sure I completely grasped that she was dying.

The days banged into each other like the clackers I played with as a kid. One day smashing away the next. Mark and I get to know the nurses, particularly a young pretty one called Kasha who has a tattoo of an owl dedicated to her daughter who died, and Meghan, who looked after us the night we arrived. They treat us gently, making us tea and answering our questions. When they finish their shifts, they introduce us to their replacements, always making sure we feel confident in their expertise. The staff at the hospice keep guard over us like soldiers posted at the castle gates. If people arrive to visit, they first must be vetted by us before they are allowed in.

Friends come, bringing us food. They sit with India, pray for her, talk to her even though she rarely stirs except when it is time for more meds and the hallucinations begin to rear their heads. Eventually even this stops, as Dr. M figures out the right ratio of drugs and the nurses figure out the timing.

Though I'm happy India is out of pain, I miss her presence. She lies on the bed, fast asleep like Sleeping Beauty. I curl into her, kissing her face or holding her hand. I bury my head into her skin, trying to memorize her smell. It works. If I close my eyes now I can still smell her, feel her hand in mine. She had the most delicious skin, half olive, half pale English Rose. When she was a baby, I used to want to eat her up. I'd put her little foot in my mouth and pretend to eat it, blow loud kisses on her stomach. I used to do this when she was a teenager and sick in bed. She'd pretend it annoyed her but then she'd forgive me and laugh.

When Yolly or Shauna visit – I can't actually recall a time when Shauna is not with us – I wander down to the little library and borrow books about grief or visit the South American woman who runs the kitchen where we can buy dinner for three dollars. I like to be in the kitchen at lunchtime when the other children are eating. Most of these children have developmental disabilities and are stuck in big wheelchairs that look like oversized prams. I'm particularly struck by one boy who isn't much younger than India but is intellectually very young. He wears a seizure helmet decorated with little paper Canadian flags. He has freckles and a toothy grin. When the nurse jokes with him, he laughs ferociously. I could sit there all day and listen to this. This sound is one of the few things that offer me solace.

One evening while Shauna is lying cuddling India in her bed, Mark and I go for a walk. Outside, despite it being evening, everything seems lit up, like a movie set, and I'm struck by how normal the world outside the hospice is. Kids play in the park, people walk their dogs, all oblivious to the tragedy unfolding in our lives. I spot a small rabbit sitting next to a shrub. Mark and I stop to study it. It reminds me of India. Six months earlier at Easter, Shauna brought her friend's baby Lionhead bunnies for India to play with. India had sat holding a little black and white one, gently stroking it, begging, "Please, please, Mummy, can I keep him?" I wanted to say yes, but I was pretty sure the creature wouldn't survive our dogs. Maybe if I'd known what the next months would bring, I would've said yes and tried to figure out something. But then I'd been tired, stuck in survival mode.

Weeks before, India's best friend, Ally, had come for a visit. They'd spent hours together up in India's room, on the narrow hospital bed, bent together, whispering. On the way back home from dropping Ally off at her foster mother's apartment in the city, India had slept across the back seat of the car while the sun set on the Gatineau Hills. Not far from our house, I'd spotted a wolf. The animal was thin, and it looked tired and hungry. "Look Mark, see, it's a wolf. A wolf, right? Not a dog?"

"Yes, it's a wolf," he'd agreed.

We'd both gone silent. The wolf scared me. It was the only creature we knew India to be afraid of. For this reason, Mark and I both sometimes imagined a wolf was her spirit animal: a force so zealous and determined to protect her that it would be frightening. I realized I was being superstitious, but I couldn't shake the feeling that this was more than a random sighting. I tried to convince myself that maybe I was being negative, that maybe it was a good omen. But the taste of the bile in my mouth told another story.

As we walked through the park, Mark and I talked about the latest development. That afternoon we'd met with Dr. M and she'd suggested we remove the bolus hydrating India. Evidence suggested its presence could increase the suffering of the dying. I'd tried my best to listen as she'd explained the facts, but I couldn't shake the feeling she was asking me to murder my daughter. I'd even said that to the doctor. She'd been gentle with me, told me I could take time to think, I wasn't to feel pressured. Nothing would happen without my consent.

"I can't do that, Mark. I can't stop feeding my child. I'm her mother."

"I know." Mark took my hand. I knew he understood the science of what was happening more than I did. "I don't know what's best either."

My friend Jenny visits us, bringing us a refrigerator full of food: cheese, olives, hummus, samosas, dinners we could heat up in the microwave. She brings a large bottle of very fine Scotch. I hide it in the bathroom, unsure if we are allowed to have it. India's old babysitter and long-time friend Sarah and I take turns taking shots of it. When Mark finally goes to have a drink, half of it is gone. He laughs at me, saying he's amazed I'm standing. The Scotch is like the rye – it doesn't make me drunk; it just softens the sting of reality.

Mark asks our nurse if we're allowed to drink. He's told we are to do whatever we need to do. So the Scotch is moved from the bathroom to the top of the fridge. Later, Anita will replace it with beer.

Mark and I are kind to each other. We never lose our tempers or behave cruelly. Neither of us blames the other. We are both rational enough to know it's nobody's fault. We share an intrinsic, silent agreement that if either of us could take her place we would. We make each other cups of tea, share cigarettes and glasses of Scotch, like two soldiers thrown into a battle they hate and have no understanding of. I no longer rant at God, nor do I beg. Both seem pointless. At least, here in the hospice, for the first time in years, I feel as if the medical system is on our side. People here understand this is war.

One night, Mark is looking out the window and he spots some of our friends setting up a candle vigil in India's honour and he calls me over. They place tea lights in glass jam jars on the sidewalk. The flames glow and flicker in the October breeze. I look out at the sight and think how their light reminds me of India's soul hovering between this world and the next.

I don't go outside very much, I don't like to be far from India, but one afternoon, I go outside to sit for a few minutes after ensuring Shauna will run and get me if India needs me. The sky is gleaming and blue, the sun hot on my head and shoulders. Not the usual weather for this time in October. I sit at the picnic table across from our apartment window and think. I still can't face the idea of removing the bolus. But part of me, my logical mind, worries she's suffering. Earlier in the day, while the nurse was giving her an injection, India accidentally hit me and when I'd cried out she'd heard me, and said in a clear voice, "Sorry, Mummy."

I want to go back in time, unwind the clock, make the hands go backwards, back before I knew that my child would die. I listen to my breathing. It sounds like I've been running. I stand up and head to the hospice. As I'm pulling open the door, I lose control of my legs. They collapse under me like a folding chair and I end up on the ground, weeping. Nancy, the admissions coordinator, spots me, runs over, and gently pulls me up.

"This is hard," she says. "And so unfair."

It's Wednesday and we've been in the hospice six days. Mark and I don't know how long we are going to be here. The staff tells us we can stay here as long as we need to. I try to imagine what it will be like if we are here in six months.

Mark and I lounge on the sofa in the living room, trying to distract ourselves with TV. Suddenly Mark feels uneasy and walks over to check on India. She's breathing very fast. He calls for the nurse. The nurse – she's new and this is our first night with her – checks the monitor that measures India's heart rate and oxygen level. The numbers are not normal. They are shockingly high. Mark knows, as he's been keeping track of them. He asks the nurse, "Is that okay? It doesn't seem right."

The nurse says, "No, that's very unusual." And she just stands there as if Mark is supposed to do something. He says, "Well, can we do something?" The nurse goes to retrieve Dr. M.

Mark comes over to me and says, "That nurse is making me extremely nervous."

Dr. M arrives quickly. She examines India and recognizes she's in distress. Her manner is confident and calm. She explains the reason for India's fast breathing and high heart rate is that her body is trying to maintain normal oxygen levels in her brain. She tells us this is because her body is no longer functioning properly; that this process is the beginning of the end and we can expect it to happen on and off. We sit with India for about half an hour until her breath returns to normal and she again looks serene.

Both Mark and I are grateful for Dr. M, but we are

both very nervous about the new nurse. We don't want to trust our daughter's care to this woman. Unlike the other nurses, she seems to be looking to us for direction.

Later we sleep with India between us, both of us wrapping our arms over her. Even though she's almost as tall as me, it feels like I'm sleeping with toddler India again. I coil myself about her, wishing I could be ingested into her like the water in the bolus. I try hard to fall asleep fast before Mark starts snoring.

I wake up with a start around midnight. I discover Mark is awake too. It's happening again. Mark and I both lie on our sides watching, willing her breath to slow down. Her breath is sour and smells of decay. We stay like this for hours, watching her. *Please don't let her die while this nurse is in charge*, I think, or do I pray? I'm not really sure. Finally, her breath slows and the thump of her heart returns to its usual beat. I fall asleep.

The next day, India is visited by all the women who have nurtured and given her the gifts that I couldn't. Women who would have influenced who she would've become as a woman and a mother: Janet, the woman who taught her to sing her name; Lisa, her art teacher; Yolly, who protected her; Sarah, who babysat her and acted as surrogate big sister; my friends Anita and Una, who shared jokes and stories with her; and Shauna, who played so many roles in her life it's impossible to name them all.

All day long, she's held by someone who loves her. Sometimes Mark and I are there. At other times, we disappear into the living room, unable to watch. The atmosphere is a mixture of hilarity, disbelief, and solemnity. How can this beautiful creature be dying? If only she would open her eyes and tell us she's just been playing a joke.

By the afternoon the bedroom is crowded. India lies in the centre of bed, encircled by these women. Her father is the only man. The ladies take turns holding her hand, petting her hair, kissing her cheek. There's always someone touching her. Though India's eyes are closed, I feel she's aware of the conversation, which is mostly about her. After all, this is a young woman who since childhood has always enjoyed listening to grown-up ladies, the girl who used to sneak down the stairs and watch my friends when I had parties. It feels a little like when she was a newborn, and my friends would stop by to admire her and coo over her.

Sometime around dinnertime, Mark and I talk to Meghan about the previous night's nurse. I tell her I don't want India to die while she's on duty, that I don't feel confident around her. Mark says the same thing, though neither of us can say exactly what makes us so uneasy.

Meghan assures us that she will find another nurse for us, someone she trusts completely. And she will stay until they arrive – in fact, she doesn't go home but goes to sleep downstairs in one of the kids' playrooms. Sadly, I can't remember the new nurse's name, but I do remember that she was from Newfoundland and that she told India she was beautiful and it was a good thing her seventeen-year-old son wasn't around because he would fall madly in love with her. I liked her for that, treating India simply as a girl, not a dying girl.

By nine o'clock that night only four of us remained with India: Mark, myself, Una, and Anita. I remember the four of us lying on the bed with her, quietly talking for a while. After that everything grows murky. Mark tells me that at one point Dr. M asked Una and Anita to leave the three of us alone. But I don't remember that. We were lying on the bed, Mark on one side, me on the other. We were holding her tightly. It reminded me of when she was a baby and we all shared a bed.

I recall the sound of India's breathing – I'd never heard her struggle like that before. It sounded like she was being chased and I worried that she thought the cockroaches were hunting her down again. But when I looked at her face she didn't look scared. I could feel her heart thudding against her chest. It was like a galloping horse. I pressed my lips to her ear, and repeated over and over that I loved her, that I was with her, that Mummy loved her so much. I have no idea how long this lasted. In my memory it seems as if it only lasted a few minutes, but I'm certain it was an hour or more. Then her breathing and her heart started to slow down and I realized she was dying. The beats between breaths gradually grew longer and longer. As this happened, I whispered in her ear, *Go now, Indy, go ride the horses, go ride the horses. Mummy loves you.* Finally, she took her last breath. It sounded like a low sigh.

Afterwards Mark and I lay there looking at her. She looked beautiful, a fairy-tale princess, no longer trapped under a terrible spell.

9

Everything at Once

As sly as a fox, as strong as an ox
As fast as a hare, as brave as a bear
As free as a bird, as neat as a word
As quiet as a mouse, as big as a house
All I wanna be, all I wanna be, oh
All I wanna be is everything at once

– Lenka Kripac,
"Everything at Once"

I'm standing inside the entranceway trying to get my bearings. It's the first time I've visited CHEO since India died. It never occurred to me that I would be here again. I've been travelling, so I'm weighed down with belongings. I have a suitcase and two heavy bags. I'm not good at travelling light.

Almost two years after she died Mark and I moved to Penticton, a small town in the Okanagan Valley. The move has been good. I no longer feel as if I'm being constantly battered by the past. There are no unexpected memories waiting to surprise me there. Not that this makes the grief disappear. It's still present, still tucked tightly between sinew and bone. But the shape has changed. It's become a thread of red regret tangling itself furiously around every new landscape and day. There's a constant wrench of what-ifs when I see something she would've liked: wild horses we spotted while driving through the mountains, fabric that I discovered in a quilting shop where I once worked called Tokyo Train Ride, the small Manga shop I found in the mall in Kelowna, the kind she would've spent hours in slowly trying to decide what to spend her money on. All these months later, I can't walk by this type of place without going in, despite the fact I used to get so impatient when we visited them together.

People think of grief as a feeling. I see it as a creature, lurking behind corners, tiptoeing down corridors, lying in wait under beds, ready to pounce. The monster that inhabited my childhood is now as real as the mutated cells living under my skin, the constant threat of chaos springing from the unknown, swift as a falcon that has spotted its prey.

As a child, I was terrified of the dark. Lying in bed, I would remember the castles I'd been to in England, imagine the ghosts lurking in them, hiding underneath my canopy bed or in my closet. Some ghosts took the form of headless knights, others were ruthless queens, hell-bent on sending disrespectful girls like myself to burn at the stake. All the incarnations were cruel. And nobody ever came to save me.

As an adult I continued to struggle with my fear of ghosts and monsters. When India was a baby and Mark worked late, I'd lie in bed, listening for any strange sounds, ready to defend my baby with my life. Of course, back then, most of these monsters took a distinctly different form. Now they come in the shape of murderers and thieves. But sometimes I'd hear the creak of the stairway or the rattle of the wind against the window and I'd find myself worrying once more about those ghosts of my childhood.

In retrospect, I wonder if these fears were some weird forewarning, a sense that all was not as it seemed. At the time I put it down to a combination of being too imaginative for my own good, and postnatal stress. But what is intuition really? Perhaps nothing more than being able to imagine the future.

My parents disagreed vehemently on how to deal with my nighttime fears. My father believed my fear to be authentic. My mother viewed it as a ploy, a tactic to avoid going to bed. But I remember the sting of the fear. It was like being bitten, a barbed bite that flooded my body with alarm and made reasonable thinking impossible. Eventually my parents found a solution. It came in the shape of a large poster of an English sheepdog with a quote that said, "A dog is the only thing in the world that loves you more than itself." I was told to look at it whenever I was afraid. This I did repeatedly, praying to that dog the way other children might to God. Oddly it helped. When the fears came, I felt as if I was not alone. Since India died, I have often wished I could find that sort of talisman again. A creature upon which to project my fear and grief.

In the early days of grief, I felt as though my body was in a different place from those who surrounded me. As if I was a parcel at the bottom of a box, under layers of bubble-wrap. I suppose it was shock protecting me from the world. Nowadays when I think of the world, I'm reminded of an old red brick rectory near where I used to live in Ottawa. The roof was covered with barbed wire and shards of glass, to keep the pigeons away I expect. I used to find this funny as it contrasted so dramatically with the pro-life signs outside the neighbouring church.

These days I think the world is a lot like that roof. Everything has become dangerous. I spend a lot of my time trying to maneuver away from the possibility of pain. Like seeing a mother and father walking into a coffee shop with their daughter, all holding hands.

It's not that I spend my time watching for disaster but sometimes when I'm with friends, my mind wanders. I'll be looking at Mark and will suddenly think, *Where will I be when you die? How will it feel when you're gone and it's only me left to remember our little girl?* It happens to Mark too. The other night, we went to a film, and I coughed and he started to cry. It reminded him of India's illness, and how vulnerable we are.

On my second or third day working at the quilt shop, I met a customer who'd just retired from nursing. A woman I work with mentioned that her daughter is a nurse and wants to go into pediatrics. "Oh," the customer replied, "but it's so awful when they die."

I smiled and let the moment pass, silently pretending to be one of the untouched. Later I thought about the nurse from Newfoundland who'd cuddled up to India the night she was dying and told her she was so beautiful that her teenage son would have instantly fallen in love with her if they'd met.

I've grown so used to not having a choice in life that I forget I still have some power. Often I just forge on. Move through the moment and hope it passes quickly. I expect this is why I'm here at the hospital, trying to figure out my next move. It never occurred to me I didn't have to come.

I'm an hour early for my appointment with Dr. Dyment, the geneticist on India's case, who has written several papers on it. I told Una when she dropped me off, my plan was to have a coffee at the cafeteria and get ready for the meeting. But now that I'm here, I feel disoriented. Here but not here.

Originally I was going to visit India's cells, but when I didn't hear back from the researcher working with them, I didn't push it. I thought I'd let fate decide for me.

When I asked Mark what it was like to see them, magnified in the microscope lens, he said it was both beautiful and horrible. "Looking at her cells was like looking at a big city at night from above," he said. This made me think of the times I've arrived in Vancouver at night, how entranced I've been by all the sparkling lights. How, when I look at them, I feel both important and completely inconsequential at the same time. I thought India would've liked to see herself like this, a flickering light amid navy blue darkness. He told me that Dr. Bennett, the researcher, said India's cells were beautiful. He said he agreed but didn't know if all cells were beautiful in the same way. For me, I can't help but believe they have to be beautiful because they reflect the dynamics of her soul.

The entranceway is busy: parents with children scurry by me, some talking frantically on their cell phones, others zipping up their children's coats, or standing impatiently in line, waiting to pay for their parking. Watching them, I recall the anxiety around this. When India was ill, we were constantly scrounging for money. The parking fees were always high, even with the discount pass.

A couple of people stand at the window waiting for their rides. The children all appear healthy. Nobody looks happy to be here. They look angry or tired, all of them desperate to leave. I don't blame them. I've only just arrived and I want to go.

I stand near the window, watch the cars slowly make their way to the front of the line, remembering what it was like to wait with India for Mark to arrive with the car. I wonder how many of these parents have imagined themselves in my position. I suspect all. For most, the hospital offers some sort of solution. For me, it conjures only memories of exhaustion and loss.

It's odd to be here without India, as if I'm peeking into a world where I don't belong. I feel like I'm an imposter, a rich Western tourist on holiday in Thailand who wants to take a tour of the slums. The difference is, I used to live here. Even now, I would be willing to return if India was with me and I could just bend down and kiss the side of her face.

Outside the air is frigid and biting, but the sky is bright. The tree that stands in front of the hospital reminds me of the bones of a hand. I remember taking India in her wheelchair to sit under it. The tree is decorated with pastel-coloured plastic beads. An oasis of sorts, only moments away from the glare of the antiseptic machinery of the hospital.

Inside the hospital the walls are covered with cheerful murals in an effort to make it look less foreboding. These always made me sad, as if it were an attempt to trick the children into thinking that it wasn't really a scary place. The way the Wicked Witch in "Hansel and Gretel" covered her house with gingerbread.

The tree, in contrast, looks as if it belongs in some child's backyard, the kind a boy or girl, like mine, might swing from. I liked to imagine who'd taken the time to string the beads around it. It was one of the few gestures of real empathy I'd encountered here.

The last time I took India to sit under the tree was on her fifteenth birthday. The air was so thick and humid I felt as if it was holding me up. She'd been in the hospital over forty days. My friend Erin was with us. She'd stopped by to give India a birthday present, a string of blue and white African beads. I remembered India smiling as Erin put them on her.

Another friend of mine, Tami, had stopped by later, with a bag of gifts that included some teen fashion magazines. Later India and I lay together in her bed and looked at them. Our shoulders touched as I held the magazine up.

At the time, I'd thought how odd it must be for India to be surrounded by all of us grown-ups on her birthday. She didn't look unhappy, but it couldn't have been the way she'd wanted it. Back then I told myself there would be plenty of other birthdays.

The hospital was a lonely place even though it was always crowded. People rarely showed concern for each other. As I wheeled India through the corridors, people seldom opened doors for us or made way for us. I'd watch strangers' eyes glide over India, then look quickly away. This made me angry. Frequently I found myself stifling the urge to scream at them. Often by the time India and I reached our destination – one of the many clinics we were required to visit – I was seething with frustration. Part of this was exhaustion. Maneuvering the wheelchair was challenging as I always had to keep guard over her. Even with the belt on she wasn't completely safe and tended to fall forward, so I had to keep one hand on her shoulder, which she hated, and was constantly trying to shrug off.

Some of the clinics were so small and crowded we had to leave the wheelchair outside, and I had to figure out how I was going to get India inside. At others the reception desk was far from the seating, so I had to run over and give our details to the receptionist, while watching India at the same time. Often I was impatient and ready for an argument. It was never like those made-for-TV movies. I wasn't the perfect mother. When I lost my temper, I seldom said the right thing. The receptionists were never moved by my plight. Invariably they responded with hostility. This generally led to some snappish reply from me, and India admonishing me for my bad behaviour. No doubt I embarrassed her. I suppose there were times she'd wished for another mother.

I gather my belongings and head inside the main building. The first thing that hits me is the air – it smells as if it's been infused with peroxide. This smell is not new here but today it feels toxic, as if every molecule in the building is instilled with it and it's off-gassing.

The next thing is how everyone seems to be in a hurry: hospital workers wearing tags decorated with cartoon characters bustle by, couples with children trailing behind them, a mum with her disgruntled toddler, an older mother pushing her teenage daughter in a wheelchair. Everyone seems to know where they are going.

I pass the coffee shop without going in, head towards the elevators and the basement corridor leading towards

Neurology. For a moment I contemplate heading there – a quick hello to India's neurologist, who I haven't seen since she died. I decide against it.

After all, what is there to say? And I'm not sure if he'd want to see me. Maybe I'm a reminder of a case he wants to forget, though my instinct tells me he was fond of India, that he enjoyed her quirky humour and intellect. She liked him as well. There was a softness about him, an emotional intelligence that set him apart from many of the other doctors. When he took her pulse, he'd hold her hand to calm her down, ask her about what movies she'd seen.

There are others I'd like to see there as well – the receptionist, some of the other neurologists. But the thought of the clinic crowded with all those children and their parents fills me with a shame I can only describe as teenage and consuming. As if I'm back in high school and being made lab partner with the boy who called me a slut in the schoolyard. It's the kind of shame that no amount of logic can wash away. It's as if I believe I somehow did something to provoke my daughter's death.

There's another part of me that feels it would be cruel for those parents to see me. As if they could tell from the way I carry myself or speak that my daughter died. I have this strange sense that my story travels beyond me, projects itself on my surroundings for everyone to see.

Suddenly I'm my teenage self again, trapped by what I think everybody knows about me. My body is screaming retreat. I turn around and head back to the front door. I have to leave. Breathe fresh air. It's like I'm the character in some sci-fi movie where they are forced to live underground after a nuclear holocaust. I've got to get out or die trying.

Outside the hospital I come up with a plan. I will visit my grief counsellor, Carol, at Roger's House while I wait for my appointment. The idea of visiting the hospice makes me feel relaxed, as if I've decided to visit my favourite auntie, the one person I know will be on my side.

At Roger's House I ring the bell and am led into the foyer by a volunteer I don't recognize. I wait, noting the knitted guest slippers I was so fond of are gone, and now, in their place, stand several rows of plastic slippers.

The volunteer beckons me into the front hall. The light in the room reminds me of candlelight. There's a party taking place in the kitchen. Laughter spills out into the hall. A nurse passes by pushing a dark-haired girl of eight or nine in a wheelchair. The girl's head flops to one side. There's something familiar about the shape of her chin. I have the urge to slowly run my hand along the line of it. I want to talk to the child, do something to make her smile. I know I can't. Anyway, the last thing she probably needs is to have another stranger staring at her.

Unlike the hospital, nobody rushes here. Everybody acts as if they have all the time in the world. Nurses chat with their charges and each other. People wander from the kitchen eating cookies and sipping cups of tea. Finally, Carol emerges from the kitchen. "I wasn't sure who you were," she says. "I couldn't figure out who I knew from out west."

"Just me."

"Nurse Meghan is here. Should I get her?"

"Oh yes."

Carol rushes off and returns with Meghan. We sit down at a little bench in the hallway. It's next to the table with the guestbook and the candle they light when a child dies. Today it is not lit, which I'm thankful for. All the rooms are taken, as they are shooting a promo for the hospice.

This place should fill me with dread – after all, it was the last place I saw India alive, but it doesn't. It's as if I'm with my best friends from boarding school, people I've known all my life. But I've only really known Carol and Meghan a brief time. I can feel the tension I've been carrying in my shoulders softening. It's so tiring pretending to be okay. Here I don't have to do that. I can say whatever I want to and they won't recoil. Outside in the real world, I'm constantly having to look beneath what people say and focus on their intention, not on the words themselves. Here, they know how to deal with the damaged. They aren't afraid of looking at my wounds.

I feel guilty as all their attention is directed on me. I should be asking about their families and their lives, but the truth is I know so little about their interests outside of the hospice. I wish I knew more.

Instead I talk about a recent visit with another grief counsellor, well intentioned and kind, but nonetheless naive. I tell them how she advised me to lay my hand on Mark's heart when he was suffering and simply say, "Hope." It's advice that might work for someone else, but which I intuitively know won't for my husband.

"Finally, I told him. I put my hand on his heart and said, 'Hope.'"

"What did he say?"

"He said, 'Anal sex.'"

They both laugh loudly.

I don't know who but someone says something like, "Good for Mark." But it doesn't really matter what they said because their laughter is really all I need. With their irreverence and ability to see beyond the bitterness and lewdness of the joke, it's like they're my friends and we're all drinking wine and being silly. I love them for understanding that life for me these days is full of sadness and sometimes the only thing that stops it hurting is a dirty joke.

Far too soon, it's time for me to go. As I say my goodbyes, I'm sad that these two women won't be part of my new life. I realize not being able to see Carol anymore is one of my few regrets about no longer living there.

If the atmosphere at Roger's House is reminiscent of a family reunion, then the Genetics building reminds me of a Bay Street financial institution. The walls and floors gleam like stainless steel. Everything is sleek and minimal. The idea of meeting with Dr. Dyment makes me nervous. I've never been good with the science of India's illness. I clench my teeth. I started doing this after India died ... or maybe shortly before. I'm not sure which but I've cracked several teeth because of it. As I enter the elevator and head upstairs I will myself to stop, but before I know it I'm at it again.

At Reception there's a line behind which patients are supposed to stand while they wait for the receptionist. If this were my first time here it would be easy to be intimidated. Luckily the young receptionist is welcoming and helpful. Still, I wander into the empty waiting room feeling as if I'm about to fail a math exam.

On my way to the waiting room I meet Dr. Boycott, a geneticist we'd met when India was first being tested for genetic disorders. I've always liked her. The geneticists are a different breed from the neurologists. India's neurologist, Dr. Sell, once called them the rock stars of medicine, the smartest of the smart. This struck me as funny. I'd never imagined that even brilliant people could be in awe of other people's skills.

I was in awe of the geneticists as well. They were like those detectives in old British black and white movies, part historian and anthropologist, part scientist. I could almost imagine them staring at a red stain on the carpet and saying, "Yes, this is a Château Lafite Rothchild with a hint of Chanel No. 5, so therefore we know it was a woman who spilt it – ah, but smell, note the scent of garlic. The wine was poisoned with arsenic."

The first time we met with Dr. Dyment and Dr. Boycott, we sat around the table talking about our families' roots. I knew this was because certain genetic disorders are more common in certain communities, but it was a language that as a writer I understood: the slow unravelling of a family story.

So when Dr. Boycott tells me she's sorry about India, and extends her hand in support, I believe it to be a sincere gesture. I understand that she really did admire my daughter.

As we say goodbye, she tells me to call if I ever need anything.

The waiting room feels more like a regular doctor's waiting room. There's a big bulletin board on the wall with posters, one from the Rare Disease Foundation with the caption, "Do you know who I am?" Another is about carrier screening information and there are the usual medical posters about the dangers of the flu.

I remember sitting here with India and Mark – how India's wheelchair had dominated the space and how I didn't think the visit would lead to anything. I stare at the empty chairs surrounding me and think about how we'd reassured India that she didn't have to be anxious about this meeting as these weren't the kind of doctors who gave exams or needles, that all we were going to do was talk.

Finally, Dr. Dyment arrives. We chat as he leads me into the same small room where we once quilted together our family history. India had been engaged that day, offering up what she knew of our family's origins. It was different when we visited Neurology; there she tended to stick her ear buds in and disengage unless she was required to participate.

The room could be anywhere, though. It's small with white walls. The kind of room that might be used to house the photocopier in an office.

Dr. Dyment and I sit across from each other at the table. There's a gentleness about him that makes me comfortable. His voice reminds me of my college boyfriend's. I take a deep breath and say, "I want to know about your work. But really I just want to understand what India had. I still don't understand her illness."

Over the past two years, I've learned how to describe India's illness to others but I still get nervous that I'm getting the facts wrong or missing something. It seems unfair to me that I don't grasp the nuances of the disease that killed my daughter. Simultaneously I wonder if this is even a possibility for me. After all, the last time I took biology was in grade ten and all I can recall is being completely disgusted by the dissection process – we were working on a cat that looked as if it had been drowned.

"Yes," he says. "Of course, I can do that." He takes out a pad of yellow foolscap and writes SMA PME at the top of the page.

"This is what India had? I thought it was PME SMA."

"It's the same thing," he says kindly.

Dr. Dyment draws two lines and places boxes on them. At the end of each line he draws a circle with a line through it. To me, they look like the end of a train track. I replay a memory: India running down the aisle of the train from Halifax to Quebec City. She's with a bunch of other children, all rushing to watch a movie in the dining car. She's ten and has just started falling.

Dr. Dyment labels these tracks Allele One and Allele Two. He then draws an X in the second box on the first allele and an X in the third box of the second allele.

He tells me we inherit two alleles, one from each parent. Two copies of every gene. So if you inherit one bad copy from your mum, you usually inherit a good copy from your dad. He says the first time they heard of the ASAH1 condition was in the late 1970s in Turkey. He explains that these parents were related so their child inherited both bad genes.

"But this," he says, "is not the case with you and Mark. India had two different mutations on the same gene. What we refer to as compound heterozygous."

He then writes the word g-e-n-e and draws a large circle. Inside that he writes ASAH1, Acid Ceramidase. This is the gene responsible for making acid ceramidase, the enzyme that India was lacking. It works as a catalyst in the synthesis and degradation of ceramide into sphingosine and fatty acid.

I've heard these terms before but they are as foreign to me as Russian. More foreign, in fact. When I was in drama school, I studied Chekov, so I'm at least familiar with

Russian names. At home I Google these terms and get nowhere closer to understanding. Even the Wikipedia page is beyond me. But what I eventually come to realize is that ceramide is an integral part of cell signalling and that it's composed of sphingosine and fatty acid.

To me sphingosine sounds like the name of a villain in a James Bond movie. I can't even figure out how to spell it. I'm too embarrassed to tell this to Dr. Dyment so in my notes, I simply write "sphing."

To illustrate how the process of distribution works Dr. Dyment draws an arrow from "ceramide" to "sphingosine" and another from "fatty acids" to "ceramide." Over ceramide there's another arrow pointing next to the word *doubled*. Next to the word sphingosine, an arrow pointing down. The drawing reminds me of a political cartoon, about some swindling politician ruining the economy. "See here," he might say to taxpayers. "See, this is driving revenue up, but over here we still have a deficit." But what Dr. Dyment is demonstrating is that India is left with too much ceramide and this affects her cells' ability to function. (All these strange facts are making my head spin. It reminds me of talking to my nephew about Minecraft.)

Under this he draws a large oddly-shaped circle with three strange prongs. This represents the outside of the cell. Later, to make sense of these, I look on the Internet at pictures of cells communicating. I'm inundated with images of cells giving each other high fives or circles with strange octopus-style tentacles.

He explains that unlike the peel of an orange, a cell's skin is very important for communication. It takes in messages and delivers them. And it's ceramides – sphingosines and fatty acids – that make up this skin.

"Is this why her brain and her body stopped communicating?" I ask.

"Yes, exactly."

It seems strange to me that my daughter, who never stopped talking, should have an illness where communication was a problem. I don't say anything but simply allow the information to sink in. I'm taking notes as he talks but it's hard, as I need to concentrate intently to understand.

Finally, after we finish the discussion of the mechanics of the disease, we talk about how rare it is. He breaks it down for me like this: So far, he says, he knows of twelve cases of SMA-PME in boys, and ten in girls. Worldwide.

When I told my mother that India had a very rare disease, she said, "Well, I always knew she was one of a kind but this is going overboard." A joke to break the tension, but terribly true.

He tells me the girls tend to die earlier, that the boys are living into their early twenties.

"Do you think this might be related to puberty?" I ask. For many years, whenever we visited a new neurologist, I made a point of telling them I believed India's illness was somehow connected to the onset of puberty. They rarely listened. I put this down to the fact that most of these doctors were men who didn't understand the complications of menstruation.

He tells me it's a good theory and certainly one worth investigating. The disease is hard to figure out, he continues, as each case is so variable and takes so long to be diagnosed. This means they aren't able to develop a history of how the disease progresses. They are hoping to change that. The ambition is that in the future, if they have a patient with intractable seizures, they will be tested for distortions in the ASAH1 gene. This way patients won't have to wait years for a diagnosis, as India did. Misdiagnosis is extremely common with rare diseases. Patients frequently wait over five years for answers.

Since India's death, I've spent many hours trying to figure out if it would've been better to know she was going to die. There are things I would've liked to have done with her while she was still stable. Like take her to Japan. Sometimes I like to imagine her there, sitting in some teahouse, drinking her cup of green tea, trying to look sophisticated, as if she were really a native. Even the mundane aspects of the culture would've delighted her: the crowded subways, the soft drink machines that sell green tea, the plastic colourful food in the windows of the eateries. Her love of Japan was completely hers alone, a signal of independence that sprung from some mysterious place in her, far from the reach of her parents' influence. A secret love, the kind that is made more precious by its concealment. Of all the things I might have given her in those last years, I would've liked to have given her that opportunity.

Of course, if we'd known earlier, there's also the possibility the doctors could've figured out treatments that would've extended her life until we had viable options. But this is all conjecture. I don't dare really think about this. Just writing these words, I feel the familiar tightening of my jaw as I mash my teeth together.

Dr. Dyment confirms what I'd always expected: there was no reason to suspect Mark and I had these mutated genes. There were no signals, no warning signs, the chance of this happening, in the millions. If we'd married other people we might never have known we were carriers. As we talk about this, I fight the urge to ask, So why? Why did this happen? I don't, though. This line of questioning is not his domain.

He also tells me that if we'd had other children there was a one-in-four chance they'd be sick as well. Though I never wanted other children, I'm surprised to find this saddens me. It's difficult to articulate why. Perhaps it's just the idea that there was never any possibility of a happy ending.

A friend once told me about a couple she'd known who'd had a daughter with a rare genetic disorder. After the child died the couple broke up. It seems that only one of the parents was a carrier – I can't remember which parent it was, so for the sake of my story I'll say the mother – and the man couldn't forgive his wife for passing the illness on. The woman never knew she was the carrier. It wasn't malicious. Still, he held it against her. I've never felt anything like that about Mark. I suppose this is because we were both accountable. It seems cruel to think in these terms. After all, how many ordinary frailties do we pass on to our children without ever considering their origin?

Dr. Dyment and I talk next about India's cells. He says they are learning a great deal from them, particularly about the nature of the ASAH1 gene. He believes they might even discover a therapy for her illness – and a related disease – because of them. I don't tell a lot of people about this research, mostly because I get tired of hearing them say that they believe this was the reason she was born. It's such a dishonest discussion for me. I can understand why people think this might be comforting, but in truth I think it says more about people's need for summation and happy endings.

Naturally, I'm proud of India but like all mothers of heroes and heroines, I would prefer my child in my arms. I can't even say that it comforts me. I don't know what to say when people tell me she has left a beautiful legacy behind. The truth is my daughter died and I just want her back. The fact that people think this makes it easier is just another demonstration of how little society understands loss. I was never asked if I wanted to sacrifice my daughter. If I had been, I would've said no. Just as I would've thrown myself in front of her if she'd told me she was going to join the army and go to war. My instinct was always to protect her. It seems to me her legacy is of more importance to others. Not to us. Not to her.

This doesn't mean I'm not happy that her cells may help other children. This pleases me greatly. I hate the thought of other children suffering as she did. I don't want other parents to go through what Mark and I have. But still, if I had a choice, I would prefer my daughter to be the recipient of someone else's sacrifice. I know this isn't noble. But it's the truth.

When Mark told me about his visit to her cells I felt jealous – not of him, but of the people working with India's cells. Jealous that they had a relationship with her, that they could read the nuances of her small existence and appreciate what they were saying. I suppose this was because she was still a very real part of their lives, and so very absent in mine. It seemed she belonged more to them than to me. This is also how I view her legacy. This gift belongs to the wider world more than it does me.

Recently, I read Robert Martone's *Scientific American* article "Scientists Discover Children's Cells Living in Mothers' Brains" (December 4, 2012), which suggests a baby's cells may remain in the mother. "We are accustomed to thinking of ourselves as singular autonomous individuals," he writes, "and these foreign cells seem to belie that notion, and suggest that most people carry remnants of other individuals."

This process is called microchimerism and has been known about for quite some time. According to Martone, it is "the persistent presence of a few genetically distinct cells in an organism." The most common way to spread these cells? The "exchange of cells across the placenta during pregnancy." Martone says, "[T]here is also evidence that cells may be transferred from mother to infant through nursing." This raises the likelihood, he points out, of "cells between twins *in utero*, and there is also the possibility that cells from an older sibling residing in the mother may find their way back across the placenta to a younger sibling during the latter's gestation. Women may have microchimeric cells both from their mother as well as from their own pregnancies, and there is even evidence for competition between cells from grandmother and infant within the mother." Evidence that we carry our families within us.

As of yet there is still much to learn about in terms of how mothers respond to these cells and what it means in the long run, but as Martone asserts in the last sentence of his article, "[I]t is also a reminder of our interconnectedness."

The article made me cry. The idea of India existing within me made me feel as if we were still fused together, that even death couldn't destroy our bond. Wherever I went in life I'd be carrying her with me and she'd remain part of my story. In the end I suppose this is my private legacy from her.

At the end of our discussion about India's cells, Dr. Dyment explains there might come a time in the future when their research is finished and they no longer need them. He says that we will naturally be involved in that discussion. It will be our choice what happens next. He says with our permission they could donate them to another research lab doing similar work. But we would have less control over them. He understands we might not want to do that. After all, everyone in charge here in Ottawa had a relationship with her.

I understand he is telling me that one day I might have to decide whether her cells should die. Strangely, when Mark visited the lab in the summer I was bothered by the idea that her cells might live for years after me. The idea filled me with anxiety, as if she were a baby and I was leaving her with someone I didn't know. But the thought of having to eventually decide to kill her cells is worse. I feel as if I'm being asked to watch her die again.

This ends our meeting. We shake hands and I make my way downstairs to meet my friend Maria, who has promised to take me to the pub for a beer. I know it will take time to digest what I have learned.

A month later, when I look at my notes from the meeting, I notice the first thing I've written is an em dash followed by the sentence fragment, *still trying to figure Indy out*. I know this refers to what the doctor is telling me about his work but it strikes me as ironic. Looking over the notes, I'm reminded of some writing I did when I first found out India had a genetic disorder and I was struggling to understand what was wrong.

The notes began, "The doctor says she's never seen anything like your cells. I don't know what she means. At the library I find a children's book with a large illustration of a cell, the different parts the colour of pastel Easter eggs. It looks like the setting of a seventies Sci-Fi movie. The Nuclear Envelope is an amphitheatre, the Golgi Complex, a rocket launching pad, the Mitochondrion where they build the weapons."

The paragraph ends like this: "This world is beyond my understanding. I am made up of the fairy tales and nursery rhymes my mother once read me. Just as you are. How could I know we would ever need these things? Often while you're sleeping I imagine I become small and enter you. I nestle against your aorta, and watch your blood choose its course. The doctors tell me that your heart is strong. Think of it as a fist, they say.

"So I picture it in my hands. After all there's nothing left now but to cling to the ferocity of its thrash and wait for the story to unfold."

All these years later, this writing still resonates with me, even though I now know the ending. It's the stories I cling to, especially on those days I can't grasp that India ever existed and that I really was her mother. I still struggle with the idea of her: how could I have a daughter and lose her? Logically I know it all happened but it still feels intangible at times, despite the evidence – the boxes of photographs and baby clothes. Often it feels as if I've lived two lives, one with India and one without. They don't seem to match each other. It's like they are pieces from two different puzzles.

But then I go for a coffee and spot some waifish teen-age girl at another table dressed like a Manga character, or a girl of eight in a purple tulle skirt, spinning around and around, and I catch a glimpse of India, feel that familiar tug.

These feelings are more than memories. They are a chemical reaction that defies my capacity for explanation, as intrinsic to my survival as my nervous system. They are proof that even now that my daughter can no longer hold my hand, she is travelling with me.

10

Where Are We Now?

It's a cold and it is a broken Hallelujah.

– Leonard Cohen
"Hallelujah"

The night sky over Penticton is indigo blue. I'm driving down Main Street towards the Skaha Lake with my windows rolled all the way down and Joan Jett blaring. It's the first week of March but it feels like June. The air is cool on my skin and I like it. Back in Quebec, my friends are bracing themselves for another snowstorm.

I'm on my way home from a meeting at the Penticton Bereavement Centre where we are starting a chapter of The Compassionate Friends, an international charity run by bereaved parents for bereaved parents. Somehow Sam, the grief counsellor, roped me into being the facilitator after I contacted her to offer grief-writing sessions. Tonight was our second meeting. So far the group has seven parents.

In Ottawa, Mark and I attended a grief group run by Roger's House. It was all couples, except for one solitary man whose wife found the group too distressing. Most of the men arrived in suits and worked in offices. The group was unusual as the genders were so equally represented. Carol, the grief counsellor who runs the group, told me it's usually a sixty-forty split favouring the women.

I don't know what grief is like for men, but if I believe the movies I get an image of a man of silent strength, willing to spring into action and fix the situation at any given moment. Bruce Willis in the *Die Hard* series, or John Wayne in *True Grit*. The men I knew in the Ottawa group were not like this. They often talked more than their wives. Mark thought they were trying to help their wives open up.

I remember the women sitting back against their chairs or curling themselves into tight balls as if they were trying to hide. I didn't see this as a male-female phenomena. Instead, I thought of it in terms of introverts and extroverts, the outgoing, more socially articulate partner taking the lead.

In our case, Mark and I both talked openly, although I have the sense that when he spoke he was fixed on India's illness and the scientific facts, whereas I spoke more about my emotions. Our different styles of mourning aren't necessarily what all couples experience, however. They are simply reflections of our personalities.

Mark is a person who measures his actions with reason. He tried to make sense of India's illness by learning about every aspect of it. Eventually he even understood the malfunction of her cells and though he found it horrifying, he could visualize what was happening inside her. Even today I still struggle to grasp the basic dimensions of her condition. I didn't know what was happening to her medically; I gauged the severity of her state in terms of her behaviours. When she no longer cared how we dressed her or no longer wanted to listen to music I understood that she was weakening.

When I asked Mark what the difference between a father's and a mother's grief was, he didn't answer the question the way I thought. He talked about the physical bonds of motherhood: how from conception mothers share a physicality with their children and how during that time the father isn't really active except to care for the mother.

Before she was born, Mark's bond with India was not yet physical, but she was already affecting his lifestyle. During my pregnancy he created a company with four other freelancers in order to have benefits and more security. He was growing increasingly concerned with making more money and acquiring status, not for himself, but for the child he already felt responsible for.

Though Mark may have lacked the physical bonds India and I shared, he didn't think this meant a father couldn't love a baby as much as the mother; he could, and did. He imagines this is a unique feature of a mother's grief, one that is hard for him as a man to comprehend intellectually. When he said this, it struck me that my relationship with India started before his. I'd never considered that before. This made me feel guilty; I wished he could have experienced what it was like to be one with her. To know that my body housed her as she grew is one of my prized memories.

From the moment India began to grow inside me, our worlds were entwined. Little by little she began to recognize the noises of my life and body. The sound of my lungs as I filled them, the rumble of my stomach, the beat of my heart. At around the seventh or eighth month she'd begin to recognize my voice and this was probably comforting. In an article in *What To Expect*, a website for expectant mothers, I learned that a fetus's heart rate quickens at the sound of her mother's voice. Certainly, she heard Mark's voice as well. But according to Janet DiPietro, a developmental psychologist at Johns Hopkins University, the fetus hears the maternal voice in two ways, as ambient sound through her abdomen as well as through the vibrations of her vocal cords. All other voices and noises are simply heard as ambient sounds. So it would seem even before I held my daughter, we were already entwined in conversation.

From the very beginning and despite our shared ideas

of equality, Mark and I played very different roles in India's life. But it was Mark who was the natural caregiver. As a teenager he babysat for a family with a newborn baby, so he confidently went about the business of parenting, changing India's diapers, bathing and feeding her. I was quite the opposite. I was terrified of dropping her, afraid of her cutting her nails in case I accidentally nicked her finger. At night, as the three of us shared the bed, Mark slept contentedly while I worried about rolling over and suffocating our newborn.

If Mark was the caregiver, I was the entertainer. I talked and talked: *See over there, that's a dog,* or *Look, Mummy's going to make herself a cup of tea,* or *Let's go sit in the garden so we can see the trees.* I played this role from her conception until the day she died.

I don't think this was particular to our genders. It just reflected our natures. We weren't unusual in this. In the Ottawa grief group, I met an older bereaved father who spoke unabashedly about how grief made him feel helpless and how he missed the daily routine of caring for his child. He was retired and his younger wife was the breadwinner. She, in contrast, never spoke, just leaned against the sofa and cried, her face buried in a Kleenex.

I doubt India rarely contemplated the roles we played in her life. She just took it for granted that if she needed bloodwork she preferred Mark's company. "You make too many faces, Mummy. Daddy's better," she would say. She was right, I never could stand to see them hurt her. Sometimes I'd even get angry, while Mark remained composed, sometimes even admonishing me for my display of emotion and reminding me that an outburst would make everything worse. There were also times, though, when he felt differently, understanding that the situation called for an outburst.

There's one particular occasion I recall Mark viewing one of my outbursts as a necessity. India had been rushed to the local hospital in Wakefield after a brutal *grand mal,* and the Emergency nurse administered a dose of Diazepam intravenously but forgot to tell India it would burn. I remember her screaming.

Pain can't always be avoided, but when the nurse basically inferred that India should suck it up, I lost my temper and told the nurse it was time she learned some empathy and that India had probably endured more pain than she ever had. My reaction seemed to have the desired effect. Afterwards she was much gentler with her.

Throughout the six years of India's illness, Mark believed it was his job to stay calm for her. It was what she needed from him. And he did this on most occasions with the studied perfection of a well-trained actor. Even in the most dismal circumstances his face never betrayed the storm of anxiety brewing inside of him. There was only one exception to this rule. This was when she had a *grand mal*. For some reason these made him panic whereas I was composed and focused on reassuring India. I don't know why this was. But my theory was I viewed these episodes as attacks on my daughter and I became obsessed with saving her.

For Mark it was different. He felt as if he was watching her sinking into an abyss he couldn't rescue her from. She couldn't speak and that scared him. He'd always been able to talk her through other medical problems. Fears raced through his mind, and he envisioned worst-case scenarios: that she'd have a stroke, go into a long seizure and end up with brain damage, or that she'd die without coming out of the seizure.

It seems to me as I write this, I'm missing the most integral person in this story: India. She always wanted me during these episodes. She'd cling to me fiercely, clutching my arms, the way she did as a toddler when she was startled by a loud noise that scared her.

During the seizures, I would hold her, whisper things like "Mummy's here" or "I love you" or "You're okay." I did my best to keep my voice even and steady. If she could just hear my voice, I reasoned, everything would be fine. I always supposed she could hear me.

I never thought about how it sounded from her perspective. Did she hear the fear? The panic?

During these times, did my voice sound like it did it when she was in the womb – far away, as if she was floating under water in a pool and I was sitting at the edge, calling down to her?

In the Penticton grief group, we only have one man. Mark doesn't come to the meetings. I don't push it. Perhaps if he hid his grief I might. Friends have told me I should. This makes me feel awkward, as if his grief is mine to manage. It's not. He has his method and I have mine. On bad days he retreats to his office and buries himself in work or plays his drums, until the endless thud of grief subsides.

The rhythm of the grief we share is so in sync that my bad days frequently follow Mark's. I'm ashamed but there are days when Mark's grief fills me with dread and even at times anger, instead of empathy. On those days I feel as though I'm seated in a roller coaster about to plunge down the steep rail. I have no energy for anyone else. All I can do in the face of his grief is tell him that I'm sorry. Mark is more adept at dealing with my sadness. He strokes my back, cuddles me – nonetheless he is unable to offer words of consolation. He never says things will get better.

It's not just the lack of men that make this group different – though that's definitely part of it. It's the atmosphere. The air in the room crackles with anger. We curse, cry, and laugh.

After our first meeting, the grief counsellor told me the group she was leading wanted to know what was going on, why we laughed so much. Some might find it shocking to imagine us laughing – after all, the first time I taught drama to a group of severely disabled adults I was surprised by how funny their caregivers were. I'm not sure why I expected them to be serious – a lack of exposure to authentic heartache, possibly? Too many made-for-TV movies, perhaps? No real understanding of how we survive? Now I see that often laughter is the only way to deal with suffering. Over the last years I've laughed at the oddest moments: a friend telling me I look good since I lost weight, or someone saying that life is still beautiful.

When I laugh at these comments, I can see in the other person's face the subtle markings of discomfort, a raised eyebrow, a tightening around the mouth, an intake of breath. It makes me feel cruel. I don't mean to be. I've lost weight because I can't eat. Food is no longer a sensual pleasure; it's just fuel. Yes, the world is still beautiful and though I can appreciate the exquisiteness of the tiny hummingbird that visits my garden, it fills me with sadness that I cannot point it out to my daughter.

Sometimes people say things will get better. I would never use the word *better* to describe my state. Things will never get better. I've adapted to that; I don't ever expect to feel the way I did while India was alive. For the rest of my life I will carry the burden of days *before* and *after* this tragedy, not just in my memory, but in every cell I possess. If I manage to quiet my mind, my body reminds me. I'm like an addict: I twitch, I scratch, I pace – I can't silence the past. I suspect the laughter is some kind of ironic spasm, an attempt to come to terms with the incongruities of my state.

I don't know where this laughter in my new grief group originates, but I suppose it's a reaction to the desperateness of what has happened to our lives – the paradox of loss, of believing somehow we were in control. But then, it could be we are all aching for an opportunity to forget, even for the briefest moment.

I suspect, though, it's basically that most of the parents in this group have to do a lot of "playacting" in real life. We pretend to our work colleagues that we don't mind hearing about their children, when acquaintances ask how we are doing we act as if we're getting better, we push through the holidays as if they have always been associated with loss. But in this group, the laughter is a sign that nobody feels like they have to pretend. We are all too aware of the grit it takes to survive.

We cry a lot too. When I listen to another mother or father whose experience mimics my own, I lose control. The mother, who has gone to sleep knowing the next day is probably her child's last. The father, who can't get the sound of his daughter's last breaths out of his mind. These encounters jolt me back in time: the way a flying stone smacking against my car's windscreen startles me from a daydream.

Many of the parents in this group have lost children to the unexpected – accidents, overdoses, violence – and some, I suspect, view me as lucky. After all, at least I knew what was coming and could prepare. They are mistaken. It was like being on a ladder during an unexpected earthquake. All I could do was brace myself for the fall. There was no way to contemplate what would happen next. I expect these parents envy the fact I had a chance to say goodbye and tell my daughter I loved her. I understand this. Even though I did these things, from time to time I worry that India didn't know how much I loved her. When I share these thoughts with Mark, he's always quick to reassure me, but still these doubts persist.

I'm tired of people searching for luck in disaster. But even I'm guilty of this type of thinking. I don't know how many times I've looked for luck in the most unlikely of scenarios. "Yeah," a friend said after I told her Mark and I were lucky we found help for India at the hospice, "you're real lucky."

Psychology Today online is filled with articles about luck: "What is Luck?"; "Make Your Own Luck"; "Trying to Explain the Inexplicable." None of these articles really told me anything new until I read Craig Dowden's "Why You Should Believe in Luck." Researchers from both UCLA and Columbia University have found that when it comes to luck, people can be divided into two groups. One believes the state is "stable," the other that luck is "fleeting." Dowden says that those in the first group think "people are generally either lucky or unlucky" and they consider themselves to be "lucky." The second group, however, perceives their luck as transitory. Luck to them is an erratic series of "ups and downs." The outcome of this is that those who believe in a steady supply of luck tend to have a considerably higher compulsion to succeed. It follows then that those who believe in the stability of luck believe they have more influence over their lives.

So perhaps my need to still believe in the possibility of luck is an attempt to grasp at the small number of things I might be able to manage. Or maybe it's an even larger attempt to take back control of my life. Either way I'm still as vulnerable as the ancient Greeks who believed their destiny lay at the hands of a group of changeable, spoiled gods.

The nature of the wounded is to make comparisons. I know this – I've done it myself. I've sat in grief groups and listened to other bereaved parents and envied them because they had other children or could still have children – as if those things are a consolation prize and somehow make up for tragedy.

This is a difficult area for me, I confess it. Common grief philosophy says we aren't supposed to compare our pain. In theory this makes sense but in reality it's human nature to compare our lives and achievements, so naturally we do the same with our losses. Is it so hard to comprehend that I might envy those bereaved parents – or any parent for that matter – with a child they can still hold and talk to? Must I feel guilty for this too? As long as I don't voice these thoughts to other bereaved parents, is it okay that these thoughts swim about in my head?

It works the other way too. Some time ago, in a grief

group, I met a bereaved mother whose teenaged daughter had committed suicide. Her face and body exuded anger. When she spoke she cut the air with her hands. I wondered if people thought this about me. In this woman's presence I was immobilized, petrified I'd say something that would intensify her anguish. Suddenly I understood how some people must feel with me.

Halfway through the session, she leaned towards me and asked if I'd had any signs from my daughter. I wanted to lie and say I hadn't. Instinct told me it would hurt her if I said yes, but I couldn't lie.

So I told her a story about how on what would've been India's nineteenth birthday, a day I find more difficult to endure than the anniversary of her death, we'd gone on a pilgrimage of sorts to the Kootenays. And while Mark went into the gas station to pay, a large crow appeared. One wing was broken so it couldn't fly but it didn't seem to be in pain, just busy snacking on something on the ground. The bird made me think of India. An art teacher of hers had told me that India had once said if she was a bird she'd be a crow. The comparison made sense to me. Both creatures were known for their cleverness and curiosity. But it was this crow's brokenness that set it apart from the other crows I'd seen on our trip. It made me think of how India used to tell me when she was old enough she was going to get a tattoo of a broken wing.

I told the woman I thought it was a sign from India.

"I haven't had a single sign from my daughter since she died," she said, looking hard at me.

That night, I couldn't stop thinking about that mother. In her company I felt lucky. Though I didn't completely grasp every nuance of India's illness, I understood there was nothing I could do to change what happened. I knew this other mother wasn't as fortunate. She would spend the rest of her life wondering what she might have done differently. I wished it wasn't so.

Tonight my plan was to talk about unexpected grief triggers with the group, but that didn't happen. Instead we told our children's stories to a newcomer to the group, a newly bereaved mother. I can now recognize the look of the newly bereaved, the wide-eyed bleary stare of loss – the look of someone who's been slapped.

Here I'm one of the veterans. Most of the others haven't even hit their two-year anniversary yet. In Ottawa, I remember crying as I listened to a couple who'd been bereaved for two years talk about their suffering. It terrified me. Two years later they seemed just as devastated as I was. *This is never going to end*, I thought. For the rest of my life I will be like a dog in a choke collar waiting to have the breath wrung out of me.

One of the parents in the group says she can tell where we are in our grief by the way we talk about our loss. She's probably right. As the months unfold, I seldom cry when I tell India's story now. It has become so entrenched it can feel as if I'm reciting some Shakespearean monologue I learned at drama school. It's not that it doesn't hurt; it's just I've grown accustomed to saying it – learned how to distance myself from the entrails of the experience.

Halfway home I stop at a red light and pull a cigarette from my pack and light it. It feels good to drive and smoke. It's been a long time since I've driven. Since we've moved out west I do less by myself. When India was sick Mark and I could rarely go out together. One of us usually had to stay home. Now we remind me of one of those high school couples, constantly circling around each other.

The speed limit is fifty but I'm doing sixty. I want to go faster. Put my foot on the accelerator and race towards the mountains and the highway. Like in some movie, where the main character runs away from their life in the big city after some defeat and drives until they can go no farther. I decide against it. It's almost nine o'clock – Mark is waiting for me and he'll worry if I'm late. Besides, my stomach is rumbling and I should do something about it. These days Mark and I survive on foods we can pull together quickly. I've lost count of the cheese sandwiches I've eaten. Long gone are meals around the dinner table. We eat on the sofa, while studying our phones or watching TV.

Dr. Bessel A. van der Kolk, in his beautiful book *The Body Keeps the Score: Brain, Mind and Body in the Healing of Trauma*, says, "Traumatized people chronically feel unsafe inside their bodies: The past is alive in the form of gnawing interior discomfort." In other words, there's no escape – all I can do is surrender to it, acknowledge the pain. I hate this – I hate grief. I hate what it has done to my life and to my husband.

I used to love food. Now, the minute my stomach fills I'm engulfed by sadness. I try to trick myself by eating quickly but it doesn't work. The only time I enjoy food the way I used to is when I have lots of company. Then I take second helpings and clean my plate off. I've dropped three dress sizes since India died. I'm not skinny – I had a lot to work with. There are certain foods that are worse than others. I used to love bread. I could eat a French stick in one sitting, but now I'm constantly throwing out moldy bread. Everything tastes as if it's infused with sugar. I still long for sweets, but if I treat myself to a donut I have trouble finishing it. It makes my jaw ache. So I eat like a toddler, existing on handfuls of crackers and mashed potatoes. When I do get cravings, I long for the British foods of my childhood: my mother's Yorkshire pudding, her sticky roast potatoes smothered in gravy, the roast beef she served on Sundays.

An old friend suggested that it makes sense I can't eat. For years I cooked for my daughter. I don't think that's all of it, though I did pride myself on trying to nourish her, especially when her carbohydrate intake was so limited on the MCT oil diet. In those days I spent hours trying to concoct the semblance of a normal meal, cutting her slices of bread so thin that it looked like she was getting more than the allotted amount and learning to bake with almond and coconut flower so she could occasionally eat a cake.

In the last months of her life, I did my best to feed her anything she wanted. I'd drive forty-five minutes to Ottawa to pick up Chinese food or Indian food if that was what she craved. Food was one way I could demonstrate how much I loved her. It was her remaining pleasure. When she was younger and I felt like treating her, I might stop off after work at the Giant Tiger and buy her some markers or a notebook to draw in, but now she had no need for these things. All I could offer was food and my companionship.

In the years when we didn't know what was wrong with India, I comforted myself with eating, feeding away the worry, or attempting to anyway. During those long hospital stays I ate greedily in secret when she was asleep so she wouldn't see I was eating what she couldn't. I ate to ward off the endless throb of the gnawing fear. Like India when she was dying, food was my only pleasure.

It didn't work. I was never full. I would gulp down a plate of spaghetti and before Mark was even halfway through his be filling up my plate again. I got fatter as she got thinner. Out in public I used to wonder what people thought when they saw India and me together. Did they wonder how that big woman could be that petite girl's mother?

I didn't go out much in those days. But one of the events of the year I looked forward to was my friend Erin's Christmas party, a boozy all-women event where we exchanged handmade gifts and drank and danced until we were exhausted.

When I'd lived in the city I would frequently traipse the five blocks home at three or four in the morning. When I moved to the country I'd crash on Erin's sofa, her little terrier Audrey lulling me to sleep with her snores. All the women dressed up for the party so I'd start thinking about what I'd wear weeks before. This grew harder as I gained weight.

I remember going to one of these parties when India was thirteen. By then, her condition had deteriorated to the point that in the mornings I dressed her for school because her hands shook so severely. Afraid to walk down the stairs, she maneuvered her way slowly down them on her bum. But I was feeling optimistic for a change. I'd bought a new dress for the occasion and when I wore it I felt beautiful. It had been a while since I felt that.

This quickly changed when, halfway through the party, an acquaintance plopped down on the sofa next to me and said, "You've gained a lot of weight. You should start exercising. If you ever want to go running I'll go with you."

I mumbled a quick thank you and changed the topic hastily. She'd hurt my feelings but I didn't want it to show. This conversation was evidence of something that I'd already begun to suspect. My life was bound by the constraints of being a caregiver. I no longer fit in my old world. There was no time for exercise. I was so emotionally exhausted if I had free time I spent it staring at the TV or joining a close friend for a beer. This woman's children were grown up and healthy; she was free. India depended on Mark and me the way she had as a baby. The luxury of caring about my appearance was gone. As for my health, I couldn't afford to think about that. Mark had gained weight too, for exactly the same reasons, though nobody ever said a word to him.

In my favourite photograph of India and me together, I'm about thirty-seven, thin, dressed in jeans, runners, and a T-shirt. India has a blonde bob, pedal pushers, and bright running shoes. She's just arrived home from kindergarten and she's giving me a hug. Her arms are so tight around my neck my face looks pushed in. When it was taken all those years ago, that wasn't what I noticed, though. Back then all I was concerned about was how big my thighs looked in those jeans.

When we returned to Wakefield to sell our house, I was reminded of van der Kolk's "gnawing interior discomfort." As

Mark and I drove around our old hometown, I was plagued with the same physical sensations I experienced in the weeks after India's death.

I purposely avoided my old house, stayed away from all the places I considered triggers, but even driving to an old friend's for dinner caused my chest and arms to ache so furiously I was afraid I was having a heart attack. In the end I had to acknowledge: the place I once considered home is to be avoided at all costs. Nothing there is safe. The physical pain began to fade the minute we headed westward on the highway towards northern Ontario. By the time we reached Winnipeg, the pain was completely gone and I was eating again.

I drive the last block towards the townhouse complex where Mark and I live, savouring the last few moments in the car. The complex is quiet. When we moved here, we joked it was like we were retiring from life. There's a pool. The beach at Skaha Lake is only a short walk away. It's like being permanently on vacation.

Most of our neighbours are older. I seldom see any children. The decorations in our neighbours' small front and backyards offer us clues to who they are: whoever lives in unit eight must really like the seaside, because their garden is covered with lighthouses and shells, and what's with all the angels in unit five, and I think unit nine must be from Alberta – they have pricey patio furniture.

At Christmas, most of the units were decorated with coloured lights and large wreaths with bold bright ribbons. We still had our decorations from Hallowe'en up. (I only took them in a couple of days ago.) In the autumn, I bought art supplies to make a wreath for winter. I made two purple felt birds, embroidered their wings in silver and yellow. I never finished. I told myself I'd make it in time for spring instead. But I've lost my impetus. When we were in the hospice with

India, I brought my sewing with me. I was making a small felt quilt with boiled blankets. It was a distraction that kept my brain occupied and my hands from shaking.

On each square there's a different piece of appliqué. There are owls, trees, flowers, a small hand. I was making it for India. I knew she was dying but at the same time I had this idea that she would one day take it with her when she went to college. The quilt was never finished. It never will be. I folded it up and put it away in the ottoman next to my bed. I don't know what to do with it.

In the townhouse, Mark and I both have offices. Mine also doubles as the guest room and is filled with crafting supplies. Over the years, I've collected jars of buttons and ribbons, wool and felt. I had a studio in our house in Quebec, but when India's condition deteriorated it just became a place to run away to. I'd turn the stereo on and dance, attempting to loosen up my muscles and escape for half an hour. After India died I never used that room again. It became a storeroom, the floor littered with dust bunnies and boxes destined for charity shops.

I don't dance in my new room. I seldom even use it, preferring to write or knit in the living room or sometimes, on bad days, in bed. The room is pleasant, though, with a large window that faces the front of the complex. But like my old room, it's a storeroom of sorts, the closet jammed with boxes filled with India's belongings. Recently I sifted through them, held a pair of her baby socks in my hand, marvelled at how small they were, remembered popping her feet into my mouth and blowing on them to make her laugh.

Later when she was a teenager and we'd lie on the sofa watching a movie, I would hold one of her feet in my hand. Not long ago, I found myself sitting on the sofa with my sister with my hand around her foot. I only realized because the shape of her foot is different from India's.

After visiting a friend whose fridge was covered with photos of his kids, it occurred to me that I could do that too. I don't know why I hadn't thought of it before. Some twisted idea that there was something wrong with doing this because she was dead. I suppose I worried it would make people uncomfortable or that they'd ask me about her. Also, I worried it would upset Mark. He still finds it difficult to look at pictures of India. I gave him a frame last Christmas but it's still in a bag on the floor of his office. In the past he was always the one who took the pictures. Now I feel badly there are so few photos of Mark and India together.

As I was sorting through the boxes in my craft room looking for photos to put on the fridge, I found a photo of Mark with India that my parents must have taken shortly after she was born. In it he's still wearing blue hospital scrubs. He's looking down at her, and it's clear by the way he's holding her he's entranced with her. She's so tiny, a little bird of a girl. The photograph is difficult for me to look at. It's not that I don't like to see India as a baby – I keep a photograph of her first breastfeeding on my fridge – but it upsets me to know I will never see that expression of wonder in Mark's eyes again.

The night India was born Mark slept on the floor of our hospital room. I don't remember much of India's birth except that eventually, after many hours of pushing, we ended up in the operating room. Recently a male friend told me how beautiful he thought the birth process was. Mark's reaction was very different. He hated watching me in pain. It wasn't a calm, beautiful experience. Somehow Mark managed to look serene when they gave me the episiotomy and pulled India out with the forceps. He'd pictured the forceps as small, delicate scissors, not a huge two-handled scythe that looked like some sort of alien instrument. He was shocked when he saw them and just started blathering, saying anything he could think of like, "You're doing well, everything's okay, it's going to be fine ..." In hindsight, I find it amusing to note how, for a short time, Mark and I exchanged roles.

It was after the doctor pulled India out of me, and after

Mark had been handed the scissors and told to cut the umbilical cord, after they'd placed her under a heating lamp, while I was lying on the operating table, that he made his oath to her. He swore to always protect her, that he would never let anything, even mere politeness or a lack of courage, stand in his way. It was the first oath he'd ever really made. He said, "I never truly understood how powerful they were before." He knew people made oaths to their countries, swearing to die, to fight to their last drop of blood, but he'd never felt that kind of allegiance, either to a person or a country. The other part of his oath, which he says was deeply significant to him, was that he promised to always be demonstrative with his love for her – to never withhold it from her – and never to lie.

He believes he failed her. He promised to protect her. "You might not understand this because you're a woman," he says, "but for a man to fail to protect someone he loves ... it's a huge failing. She was so new. I'd never seen anything so new. She was like a bud you see on a tree branch, or a new fern leaf. She was just so *new*. She radiated it."

The townhouse is the newest place Mark and I have ever lived. All our other homes were old. When we first moved in, we marvelled at the closet space, the fact we could take a bath and do laundry at the same time, that our home wasn't continually speckled with one-hundred-year-old dust.

India would've loved this place. She always hated our taste in houses. Whenever we drove in the suburbs she would point to big houses and say, "That's the kind of place I'm going to have one day."

From the bedroom balcony I can look into my neighbour's backyard. Today there were six deer, standing around as if they were having tea. A large male deer stared at me as if daring me to take him on. I can also see the creek that runs along the neighbouring mobile park, watch the blue herons. In the distance I can see the mountains that hem Penticton in. They remind me of thick castle walls. At night from the balcony I watch the planes take off and fly over them and wonder where they are headed.

In August when we moved here, Mark and I used to sit out on the patio and drink a beer as the sun slowly sank down. Mark rarely drank before but these days he often joins me. In the past he preferred to get his sugar from ice cream. Now he drinks – Scotch, beer, rye, never a lot, always what I call medicinally.

I have a memory of us in bed, drinking rye, not saying much. It's very late at night. India is asleep in her room down the hall. Our room is dimly lit and untidy. There are piles of clothes on the chair by my bed. We are both aware that our daughter is dying. We speak in hushed tones as if we're in a church. We are afraid of waking her. We don't know what to expect if this happens. Will there be more hallucinations or will she simply turn over and fall asleep again? I drain my glass, the alcohol warming my throat as it goes down.

"You drank that quickly," Mark says.

"Yes," I say, grab the bottle, and pour myself another.

The grief is still with us here. It follows us from room to room, lurks in the space between us as we sit on the sofa. We live a see-saw existence from bad day to good day. During the month of October, both before and after the anniversary of India's death, I felt as if I was losing the battle. The sadness inhabited my body; it felt as if I was walking around carrying piles of bricks in my arms. All I could think was I didn't want to live like this anymore. It was the same for Mark. The grief in our house was as palpable as humidity in the ocean air.

Then it cleared. I don't know how or why. Nothing particular happened; there was no magic potion, no epiphany, no bright light. Mark bought himself a drum kit, I took a quilting class, we tried to live, all the time knowing that the grief was waiting, a sniper hiding in the long grass.

When India died it took ages for Mark to get used to

being away from our house. When she was sick and he was away he was always anxious to get back to her. He carried his phone with him all the time in case we needed him. "It was a kind of mania," he says now.

For me, it was the opposite. On the days I worked, I found the drive home unbearable. While away, I'd forget she was sick or at least imagine her illness had changed shape and she wasn't as sick as she was. Driving up the hill, past the horse farm with its apple trees and kids playing in the fields, I'd clench my hands around the steering wheel, push the accelerator with my foot, knowing I needed to get home and give Mark a break, but at the same time screaming because I was scared of what I'd discover when I got there. The pit of my stomach stretching and contracting like dough under a rolling pin.

Often, I cried the final stretch of the drive home, my face sticky with snot and tears. That was okay, I could cry in my car. There was nobody to hear me, only the crows and the carcasses of dead raccoons on the side of the road. When I pulled up into the driveway, I would brush my face with my hands and try to prepare for the sight of my dying daughter, whose image never matched the one I carried with me – the girl who was healthy and perpetually moving.

One of the ironies of my situation is that Mark and I are free to do whatever we want with our lives now. There is nobody to be responsible for, nobody to leave an inheritance for. We have the freedom we had when we first met, only now it's the Janis Joplin kind: nothing left to lose. This freedom is wasted on me. I would rather return to the past, and be caring for my daughter. I don't know what to do with all this time I've been given. It seems empty without her presence.

Mark and I met twenty-two years ago at a Christmas party called The Jane and Jane, held annually by two friends, both called Jane, in an Ottawa Curling Club. It wasn't love at first sight but it was a dramatic beginning.

"Mark has a broken heart," his friend said when he introduced us.

"Oh, does it hurt?" I asked, pressing my finger into the flesh where I thought his heart should be. In hindsight this beginning strikes me as ironic. What did either of us really know of heartbreak? I suppose we thought we did. He was thirty-six and I was twenty-seven. My first impression was that he was too old for me. He was practically forty. Besides, he wasn't my type, which was tall, lanky, arty, and underemployed.

We were no longer babies. My Australian boyfriend and I had broken up a year before after I'd discovered he'd been having affairs. I was bitter but I was intact, still able to contemplate a huge future despite being off men. I was single for the first time in years.

Naturally I didn't know back then that Mark and I would get married or have a child, and that I'd one day look back at my time with the Australian as an adventure or a learning experience. True heartbreak isn't like that. It renders the future unimaginable.

There are things and people in my life that make the unimaginable endurable: my insatiable desire for travel – there are still countries I want to visit, not just for myself but my daughter – driving fast in my little car with my music blaring, a new album by The National, my friend Patti's artwork, dirty jokes, a full glass of good Pinot Noir, and the companionship of those I love. Of all of these, I suppose it's friendship I cling to for hope. On the bad days just knowing I have an appointment with a friend can keep me from succumbing.

I've made a friend here, Michelle. She's a grown-up version of a girl I would've been friends with in high school. There's an openness I admire about her. It's in her eyes, a confidence that comes from understanding herself. Once a week we go on walks along the Kettle Valley trail with her dog and look down on Lake Okanagan. We walk briskly. Michelle is trying to get in shape for her son's wedding.

Afterwards we go to our favourite coffee shop, sip coffee, and talk. She knows about India. On one of our first outings together she asked me if it was okay if we talked about her.

"If I say anything stupid you have to tell me," she said.

She's not the first person to say this to me but I appreciated it. When she said this, I was aware there were people who might not be as emotionally open as Michelle, who might balk at the idea of being friends with a bereaved mother.

"There's not much you could say that would upset me," I said. "I'm just not good with that 'everything happens for a reason stuff.'"

"I won't do that," she promised.

Instead Michelle asks me about what kind of person India was, what she was good at, about India's obsession with Japan. This allows me a freedom I'm no longer accustomed to: the opportunity to talk about my daughter, not her death.

When I was preparing for the first meeting of The Compassionate Friends I was concerned about finding the right notebook to use as the guestbook. Finally, I settled on a book Ally had given me for Christmas that was made to look like an antique. It seems a small thing to worry about but I'd read in the literature that when parents signed into the group, they were to write their child's name as well. This was important as bereaved parents seldom get to do this.

I sat down and started writing India's full name over and over. I remembered how I used to like to write her name with a huge loopy "I". It made me feel good to do this. When Michelle asks me about India it's as if she's allowing me to write her name. It's a gift – I don't mean that in a pseudo New Age way – I mean it's like she's actually giving me a present. For a short while, I'm a mother again, bragging about my girl.

Last week at coffee with Michelle, I talked about Mark and me. The catalyst for the conversation was about people who only can see things as black and white in life. "I can't understand people who don't see grey," Michelle says. "There are so many grey areas in life."

This reminded me of the assumptions people make about grieving couples. Society only seems to recognize two scenarios. Either the couple is estranged or a great comfort to each other. I find this simplistic. Grief shifts people.

"It's not easy," I tell Michelle. "It's hard to watch someone you love in pain and know that you can't change it. There are times I wonder if we can truly be happy again. In some ways it might be easier if we hated each other. But we love each other and he's the only person who completely understands. Nobody else knows what we went through."

"See," Michelle says. "More grey."

Mark doesn't have a friend like Michelle, although that's nothing new – he's always been a solitary creature. Nonetheless he writes India's name in his own way. Every morning the first thing he puts on is her old necklace with the jade wolf charm. At night before he slips into bed, he kisses it and hangs it on the bedpost. This ritual reminds me of the way some devout Christians kiss the cross.

A month ago, Mark and I came back from the movies and as soon as my head hit my pillow I began to cry. I have no idea what triggered it but I'd been sad all evening. Every time I tried to close my eyes and go to sleep, the sadness just seemed to become more aggressive. In the end I was howling. It was like the first few nights after India died.

My skin felt as if it was tightening around my skull. The pit of my stomach ached as if I hadn't eaten for days. It felt like when I'd had gum surgery and the painkillers were wearing off, only it was my entire body and all my nerves were raw. Mark tried to comfort me; he stroked my face, cuddled me, held my hand. Nothing worked. From time to time he would cry as well, in part because he felt helpless in the face of my grief but also because he understood my pain. Then he would sob for India – loud, hard cries that made my ears ache. But mostly he was there as my caretaker, trying his best to soothe me. I remember him repeating, "I know, honey. I know. I'm so sorry. It's not right this happened to us. I'm so sorry."

I don't recall being concerned about Mark that night. I never considered what my grief would trigger in him. I just remember clinging to him, needing him the way a child longs for a parent when they have a fever.

After several hours, he said, "We could go to Tim Hortons and get you a hot chocolate and go for a drive."

So at three a.m. we got out of our bed, got dressed, and headed to the car. I didn't instantly feel better but the howling stopped as soon as I had something to focus on. The night air was chilly. I didn't mind – it was like jumping into a cold lake when you have a sunburn.

As we drove towards the coffee shop, I looked at the empty streets. It was strange to be awake when the town was sleeping. I thought people would think we were crazy if they knew we were out at this time of night.

After I got my hot chocolate we headed towards OK Falls, down my favourite road by the lakeside with the curves that remind me of the south of France and the fancy houses we can only dream of owning. In the distance, I could see the lights of the town. Against the dark sky, the lights made the small working-class town look exotic, like some South American city on the ocean. Everything was transformed by the night: the lake was suddenly an ocean, the tumbleweeds grey ghosts somersaulting down the hills, the tall fence posts guards asleep on the job. Once we reached the town, it was re-formed to its usual state and so was I. The blackbird of grief had taken flight – for now.

We drove back to Penticton on the highway past thick wooded areas, another landscape entirely, this one belonging to Grimm's fairy tales and witches. We made quiet conversation about this, pointing out how it was like being in another country on this side of the lake.

When we got home, I fell asleep easily, my leg touching Mark's.

11

Refuge

So we can be filled with holes and loss and wide expanses of unhealed geography — and we can also be excited by life and in love and content at the exact same moment.

— Augusten Burroughs,
This Is How:
Surviving What You Think You Can't

On the Vancouver to London flight, I'm surrounded by a group of middle-aged women photographers, heading to the Scottish Highlands with their instructor. I'm in the aisle seat. The instructor is seated by the window and her companion is in the middle. Her other students are seated in the two rows behind us. They're from a small town in northern British Columbia that I've never heard of. None of them have ever been overseas before.

The photographers reach over me to chat with their instructor, ask questions about their schedule, talk about what they want to buy or see first. They take photographs, laugh, raise their glasses as they toast the trip. I'm moved by their eagerness. It reminds me of the thrill of going to summer camp as a child.

From time to time, I hear the instructor, who seems younger than her pupils, chat with her neighbour about her daughters. I can tell by the tone of her voice she's worried about leaving them. I listen, wishing her worries were my own. How normal they seem. I wonder if she can sense my envy. Loss makes the mundane extraordinary in a way that's unimaginable to those untouched by it. It makes one long for the ordinary.

Four years have passed since India died. It's April 2017, and I'm on my way to the Shetland Islands, a Scottish island chain northeast of England renowned for its Viking heritage and textile traditions.

Around my neck on a thick silver chain is the last Indy bead. I can feel it pressing against my collar bone. It's red glass, about the circumference of my wedding ring, with a silvery-white swirly flower on it. I've been wearing it a lot lately. I don't really want to let go of it but I believe it's time.

Along with this, pressed in my notebook is a photo of India as a newborn. She's swaddled in a baby blanket and wearing a crocheted green cap. She looks sleepy and grumpy, as if she wishes whoever was taking the photo would just hurry up. I bring the photo wherever I go but I rarely look at it – I merely need it to be there. A physical reminder that she's with me. Not that I need anything concrete to summon her. As soon as I close my eyes I can picture her at any age.

I've been invited to Shetland by my friend Fiona Duthie, an up-and-coming Canadian fibre artist. Fiona's mother is from Shetland and she's connected to the island through her family. She's staying at an artist residency in a town called Scalloway. Like Fiona, my family's roots are in the U.K. We emigrated when I was a baby but I'd spent a great deal of my childhood visiting relatives. I'd been travelling across *the pond* since I was three months old. This is a route I know well.

In Shetland I'll write about the new work Fiona's creating and the week-long workshop she's giving in Lerwick.

Students are coming from England, Canada, the States, and Australia. She's planned excursions all around the island to visit historical and natural sights of interest.

After the workshop Fiona has booked us a short stay in the lighthouse featured in one of the episodes of the TV mystery series *Shetland* based on the Ann Cleeves novels. All I know about Shetland is what I've learned from the TV series. So far I've figured out that it's freezing and there are very few trees. One of the ways I persevere these days is by binge-watching murder mysteries. I've even watched some, like *The Killing,* twice. I've lost count of how frequently the murdered victim is a teenage girl.

It's not the violence I'm attracted to. It's the grief. These mysteries offer me the truest reflection of my own feelings. Unlike the "based-on-true-life" stories about children who die, there are no grand epiphanies, no resolution all beautifully wrapped up. In mysteries the characters mourn unapologetically, their lives narrow. Like me they're startled by loud noises and the unexpected. I'm comfortable in this milieu. Here nobody ever says, "It all happened for a reason" or asks the mother to be thankful her child is no longer in pain. Here everybody recognizes it was better before.

In three days Fiona has promised to pick me up at Sumburgh airport. First I'll take the train from London to Durham, the town where I was born. There I'll be met by Aunt Edna and visit family before taking the train to Edinburgh and flying to Shetland.

Since India's death my trips overseas have all been to places connected to her. It's my first to the U.K. in over ten years. This trip is for me.

My instinct is still to place her before me even after her death. I'm going to have to learn how to look after myself if I'm going to survive.

Fiona and I have been working together for about a year, though we've been connected for ages through mutual friends in Ottawa. I've come to think of her as my fairy godmother, always showing up when I'm in need. This time is no exception.

In February, Mark and I bought a house in Penticton. This time we'd made a practical choice – no more old houses. This was built in the late '80s and has a rental suite. I like the house, but the upheaval of moving again elicits another bout of severe grief.

Most of the belongings we moved from our rented condo were India's – we didn't even have a sofa – six huge Tupperware boxes of drawings, colourful T-shirts, purses, lacey dresses, fingerless gloves, bottles of nail polish, and books. Neither Mark nor I have any idea what to do with these possessions. We can't bear to look at them yet we can't stand the idea of giving them to a charity shop. So they sit in the garage.

Our new downstairs' tenant has two little girls. Like my daughter they are both named after places. The eldest is a serious-faced child of about ten. Her mother tells me she has a passion for Japan just as India did. She is well-behaved and never ventures upstairs to our apartment. Often I think about giving her something Japanese of India's but I just can't seem to do it. I'm not sure if it's the act of giving it or the idea of going through India's things.

The younger sister, who is only six, has snuck up the stairs to visit us several times. I like her broad grin which hijacks her entire face. Sometimes I hear the girls calling their mother or arguing with her. The small family is only staying with us temporarily. They're supposed to be moving to Kamloops by the end of June. I feel torn, both wanting them to go and hoping they'll stay. I hate hearing the girls call for their mother but love listening to the little one laugh.

On the outside I appear to be coping better. It's all a façade. I've just become a better actress – so much so that sometimes I can convince myself for an hour or two that I'm fine. Most of the time I feel beaten. I'm struggling to picture a future for myself. Who am I without India?

I order a glass of red wine from the air hostess and take a long sip, enjoying the taste of alcohol and trusting it will make me sleep. It's after eleven p.m. I wonder if Mark has arrived home safely in Penticton. The drive isn't easy; it's filled with steep twists and turns. I remind myself to text him the first opportunity I have. He's an airplane buff and I'd guess he's envious of my flight from Edinburgh to Shetland because the route has a reputation for being challenging. My destination, however, doesn't interest him. He hates the cold. It's the other way around for me. I hate flying.

Exhausted, I close my eyes and try to sleep, listening to the murmur of the surrounding voices. All night long, window blinds are raised and lowered as the photographers admire the light or absence of light.

On the tube to King's Cross, I feel wide awake despite the fact I've only slept about two hours. I'm in my favourite city again. The first time I came here by myself I was seventeen. I stayed in a B & B near Sloane Square for three days, surviving on my breakfast of cornflakes and buttery toast so I could spend my money on clothes.

Several years later it's where I first became an independent adult – a young woman who'd moved to a city where she knew nobody so she could study theatre, who'd exhausted a week's lunch money on a night of dancing in a fancy West End nightclub, and spent her Saturdays alone at the Tate Gallery gazing at the Pre-Raphaelite paintings. I'd come of age in London. After college I'd stayed three more years working in restaurants and bars.

I often compared my love of London to being in love with the wrong person. On one hand I love London more than anywhere else – where else can a person just walk the streets for entertainment – yet on the other hand, it's a love I couldn't afford. It was way too expensive.

Though the billboards on the walls are illustrated

differently they're still selling the same products as when I lived here: theatre, booze, the best ways to send money home, cheap flights to southeast Asia, Africa, Australia – only now Eastern Europe is part of the mix. I read them enjoying the sly British humour.

The air in the tube smells of old crumpled newspaper, tobacco, and oil. I breathe in deeply, revelling in its familiarity. I remember catching the last tube home after my shift in a restaurant just off Oxford Street, all that noise and energy – young men singing football anthems, groups of women with big hair holding each other up, their spikey high heels clattering on the platform as they scurried for their trains, the late-night buskers strumming the Beatles or the Stones on their guitars, as tube goers pitch fifty- and ten-pence pieces into their collection.

I break the cardinal rule of tube travel and look at the other commuters instead of staring at my feet or phone. I smile at a little girl in a blue gingham school uniform, eavesdrop on elderly women with overflowing shopping bags chatting, watch two Japanese tourists nervously study their map, and follow people rushing in and out of the train, admiring the musicality of the city's constant motion.

At King's Cross I trail behind the commuters into the train station. Of course, I can't help thinking about the last time I was in London with Mark and India. She was only nine and it was shortly after Christmas; we took her to Hamley's so she could buy herself something in the sales. It took her ages to decide. In the end she bought these eccentric little bunnies who came with their own miniscule furniture. She was constantly leaving the furniture on the floor. I can't remember how many times I stepped on one of the tiny chairs or tables. I'd cry out with the shock, lose my temper.

What would she want if she were alive now? I know she'd be begging me to bring her back something fancy. A straight pencil skirt covered in a bold '80s print, big garish earrings, pointy red shoes or flowery Doc Martens, a green leather jacket to match her eyes. I'm certain it would be cutting edge.

I'm an hour early for my train so I head for the coffee shop. In the lineup I listen to two women in their twenties gossip about a colleague in their office who they're angry with. I don't get all the details but I do manage to find out she said something they don't like at the last office pub night.

At the mini Marks & Spencer's I buy a Coronation Chicken sandwich for the journey and sit outside so I can people-watch. Office and shop workers gather in groups, smoking, and drinking coffee. Travellers sit with their bags between their knees, texting madly on their phones, lovers hold hands, a mother whizzes past with a stroller while two young slender African men meander by. There's so much to watch that the hour passes before I know it and I'm soon heading for the train.

As I take my seat by the window I make a silent prayer that nobody will sit next to me. I'm enjoying my role as observer. When I was in college in London I'd often taken the train to visit my relatives. Back then, the train was a luxury. I'd sit by the window, drink a tea or a beer depending on my finances. I follow my old custom and treat myself to a tea, watching as the train slowly disengages from the tangle of London's suburbs.

My compartment is only half full even though it's late afternoon on a Friday. The majority of travellers carry shopping bags filled with goodies from Marks & Spencer's, Selfridges, Debenhams, Topshop. Men and women dressed for the office slump down in their chairs snoozing, kids play games on their parent's phone, an elderly lady knits. Conversations hum softly around me.

Through the window I watch as we pass: Peterborough – Grantham – Newark – Doncaster. I say the names in my head, trying to memorize each stop. It reminds me of the

Robert Louis Stevenson's poem "From a Railway Carriage." My mother used to recite to me as a child. "Faster than fairies, faster than witches, Bridges and houses, hedges and ditches."

The landscape is slowly transforming from the green meadows of the south to the rougher hills of the north. The weather is changing too. When we left London it was sunny. It's getting greyer the further up north we travel.

At York I stand up and stretch my legs, lean against the window hoping to catch a glimpse of the city. I can't remember how far the station is from the centre of town. In the past York always signalled the journey was nearly over. This was always bittersweet. Though I was always happy to see my aunt Edna, I loved the train so much I was saddened when I reached my destination.

I'm still not sure where I will place the last bead, though I have ideas. There's a paddock a short walk from my aunt's house. When India was three, she used to feed carrots to the pony who lived here. Then there's St. Michael and All Angels, the twelfth-century church where I was christened and my grandparents are buried. If those don't feel right, I could just take it to Shetland and throw it off some cliff into the Atlantic Ocean and let it be carried away by the Norwegian Current all the way to Greenland. I feel like India might appreciate the drama of that. It's strange to be making this decision on my own. Usually Mark and I determine where the beads are placed together. I hope he doesn't feel I've taken over.

I check the time on my phone. It's five p.m. With the eight-hour time difference that makes it one a.m. at home. Even if he does, he's probably not worrying about it at the moment – most likely he's fast asleep.

The train pulls into the station at Durham and it begins hailing. Still, when I look out the window and catch sight of the Norman cathedral perched high above the town, I gasp. It's been so long I've forgotten its splendour.

The stately towers with their crown of spirals. Until now it's never occurred to me to imagine what it might be like for a stranger to see this view for the first time. I've simply accepted its beauty the way one recognizes the colour of their mother's eyes or the sound of her laughter.

As a child I was much more concerned with the bronze cathedral knocker, with its intense face. Sometimes it resembled the sun, or a lion, at other times an angry Celtic spirit seeking vengeance. It was fascinating and terrifying with its hollow eyes, long arrogant nose, and curly wild mane. My favourite part was the history behind it. Until about the sixteenth century, an outlaw seeking refuge could go to the cathedral, rap on the knocker, and receive thirty-seven days of asylum. Specific monks were in charge of looking out for sanctuary seekers. When they spotted someone, a bell would be rung and the fugitive would be led inside. As a child I loved history, and used to make up stories about these outlaws. I created elaborate scenarios about young thieves or cruel masters being murdered. Once my characters received sanctuary the fantasy usually ended. I didn't really care what happened after that. I liked the drama.

Back then it never occurred to me that thirty-seven days wasn't a very long time or that the custom was designed to give both the accused and the prosecutor a chance to make amends with the disgruntled party, face the charges, or make plans for an escape. Now it seems significant. Over the past four years refuge has arrived in many guises – travel, art, study. None of them offer a permanent solution, only short reprieves. Enough time to gather strength before another stretch of longing.

I step out of the train and onto the platform. The sky is dark and hostile, the air imbued with the smell of industry and rain. Light from the station pools in the puddles. It's freezing. I spot my aunt Edna and run toward her, shivering. She quickly unlocks the car, assuring me there will soon be wine and food.

I look out the window and watch as the car twists its way from Durham towards my aunt's home in Langley Park. We zip past small villages with row houses, pubs, open fields, and churches. The rain makes everything look streaky like a wet watercolour painting.

When we reach my aunt's house the rain has stopped. I gaze up at the dark sky, marvel at the brightness of the stars before following her into the house.

My aunt Edna and I eat lasagna around her small dining table. Scattered around her house are photos of her nieces, nephews, and their children.

Over the fireplace hangs a large painting of the cathedral, the iconic view from across the river featuring the old stone mill. The house is filled with things I remember: my grandmother's crystal animals, figurines of girls, and little Russian boxes.

The last time I was here was with India. She was only three. She had golden curls and sang all the time. I don't know why but I don't feel overwhelmed by this. In fact, I'm feeling good. Today I've felt a little like my old self. My aunt is my mother's twin. She never married or had children. We've always been close. When I was a little girl she had an MG and I used to love driving in it with her. One time when I was two or three, my mother and I arrived in London, and my aunt picked us up in it. I sat in the tiny back seat all the way to Durham.

When I was a teenager, I went to Spain with her. On that trip she brought three other teenage girls plus my sister, who was ten. Not many adults would've chosen this group as holiday companions but she liked our company. She'd been a PE teacher and was used to teenagers, so she didn't take our moods or behaviour personally. She had very few rules. Actually they were more directives than decrees: "If you go on the beach with a Spanish boy after midnight you better be prepared ..." Needless to say I never tested the rule out. Instead I stayed at the disco with the rest of her teenage charges, dancing and drinking sweet bubbly wine.

When I was at drama school I used to visit her on my holidays. We'd have a curry and chips from the local Chinese restaurant and hang out watching old movies. Sometimes we'd go to the big shopping centre at Metrotown or go into Durham or visit some historical place.

As I headed back to London she'd press a ten-pound note into my hand, saying, "Treat yourself to a drink." I was always grateful for the money. In those days I survived on very little, and ten pounds was a fortune to me. It meant an extra cup of tea at the café, a pint or two at the pub with friends, and the biggest luxury of all, a block of old cheddar cheese.

We finish our dinner and move to the seats around the fireplace. She brings the bottle of white wine with her and tops up my glass.

Suddenly I say, surprising even myself, "I brought the last Indy bead with me. I wasn't sure where I should leave it but I think I'd like to put it with Grandma and Granddad. Would you come with me?"

"Yes," she says. "Of course I will."

Even though I haven't spent a great deal of time over my decision, it feels right. I'm happy my aunt will be joining me. I didn't really like the idea of doing it on my own. I wanted someone to be there as a witness. My aunt is the perfect choice. Instinctively she seems to understand how much I love to talk about my daughter and often brings her up in conversation.

I finally crawl into my bed around midnight. As I fall asleep I find myself wondering why it's taken me so long to get back here.

When I wake up in the morning, the sun is streaming through the curtains. I get up and look out at the day. The sun is shining and the sky is a remarkable robin's egg blue with bold white clouds. I contemplate my view of the street, the green hedges, the white stucco house, the fading daffodils, and the little patches of green.

I admire my aunt's collection of little chairs on her bureau. She's had them since I was a little girl. I can remember playing with them. I dress quickly, eager to start my day. I wear jeans and a long-sleeved T-shirt with a cardigan. It may be sunny but it might not be warm. This is the North. The weather can change at any time without warning, but I'm hoping it will stay sunny.

My aunt and I make our plan for the day while we drink our coffee. There's not much time and I have three aunts to visit, one cousin and a new second cousin to meet.

I understand that this day will pass in a flash so I do my best to focus on my surroundings as we drive from one engagement to the next. I don't know when I'll be here again and I want to make sure I memorize everything. We stop at my great-grandmother's childhood home so I can admire the small stone cottage with its red brick roof and garden filled with forget-me-nots. I take photos so I can show Mark. I feel a flash of regret that I never told India about this house. When I was sixteen I'd gone for a walk and I'd fallen in love with it. I had no idea it was connected to my family. When my grandmother told me, I'd decided it was destined to be mine one day. All these years later I still loved it.

After lunch with my aunt Liz and my cousin Fiona and her son, Stephen, at a local pub, Aunt Edna and I head to St. Michael and All Angels, the church where my grandparents are buried. As Edna parks her car in the lot I glance across at the farmhouse near the church. It was once a leper hospital. Ever since I was a child I've found the arch of the stone medieval window at the side of the building intriguing.

I look over at the moss-covered stone wall surrounding the church and pass under the lychgate with its red roof and wait for Edna. Long ago this little building was used to shelter the coffin, while the funeral party waited for the minister to join them. For eight hundred years this small stone church, with its sharply slanted roof, has stood here. I imagine I share DNA with many buried here.

Ancient moss-coated gravestones stand next to glossy new ones decorated with flowers. I linger to read a time-worn headstone with a face carved into it. It takes me a few minutes to realize the face is supposed to be Jesus's. The marker is so old the thorns in his crown are eroding. Above the names are the words "Affection and remembrance of the children of Thomas and Ann Ellison's of Old Waldridge."

There are five children in all, four girls and one boy. The first death is in 1869 and the last in 1896. The youngest an unnamed stillborn girl, the oldest a girl called Margaret, just thirteen years and three months old.

I note how precisely the children's ages are recorded, as if each month of their lives marks an accomplishment. The stone is big but by the time the parents' names were added at the end there was barely room. The writing is a third of the size of the original script.

I wonder how Thomas and Ann continued after all this loss. There's a name after Ann's. It's difficult to make out but it looks like another Ann – another daughter named for her mother. I want to believe she lived until she was an old lady and told everyone about her sisters and brother.

We head down through the graveyard to the hillside where my grandparents rest. Everything is shrouded in green; even the trunks of the trees are tinged with it. It makes them look as if they've been spray painted. Nearby there's a wooden bench facing a farmer's field that can be spotted through the trees. I remember walking through it with my mother as a child. The last time I was here was at my grandmother's funeral over twenty-five years ago.

Aunt Edna stops at their grave and I join her. I ask her to hold the bead so I can take a picture – I want to document the moment. She then tucks it gently under some earth at the front of the grave, carefully rearranging some leaves so it's hidden. For now, this is the final bead, the only one designed not to be found – though I like to imagine perhaps a future archeologist finding it and marvelling at its meaning and how it got there. This is a good place for my daughter. Although she never knew her grandparents, I'm sure they would've liked her and she would've liked them. Sometimes, when I looked at India I'd catch a glimpse of my grandmother in the arch of high cheekbones, my grandfather in her fearlessness.

We walk slowly back up the hill towards the church. Tomorrow morning I will be heading on a train up the coast towards Edinburgh. Later in the afternoon I will fly to an island where I've learned there's a place you can pitch a stone past land from the North Sea to the Atlantic Ocean. I like the idea of this. There's something mythical about this image. It conjures up pictures of legendary realms connecting one world to another, gateways between the past and the present. Perhaps it will come to represent a point of connection between the woman I was when my daughter was alive and the woman I'm hoping to become. I'm optimistic. This doesn't mean letting go of my daughter. It just means carrying her with me.

Acknowledgements

M any, many thanks to the wonderful doctors, nurses, and countless other health care professionals who cared for India at The Children's Hospital of Eastern Ontario, The Hospital for Sick Children, and Roger Neilson House.

I owe a debt of gratitude to the friends and strangers who supported my family with fundraisers, cards, food, letters, phone calls, and endless acts of generosity, particularly Chris MacLean, and Don Monet and Becky Rynor. Whenever I worry that the world is no longer a kind place, it's these acts I remember.

If it weren't for the early encouragement of Lorri Neilsen Glenn, I would never have applied to the MFA program at the University of King's College. I can't thank her enough for leading me there. A big thank you to everyone at King's, particularly Stephen Kimber, David Swick, and Donald Sedgwick. Thanks for your generous backing. I thank Kim Pittaway for her generous and intelligent counsel. My education has grown from it. Let me also thank Tim Falconer for encouraging me to approach Hazlitt and Valerie Howe for bringing my story to *Today's Parent*.

Whatever talent I own has been refined by the marvellous Jane Silcott. Thank you for giving so freely of your many gifts. This book was much improved by your wise advice, humour, and support.

Thank you, Sue Harper, for encouraging me to enter the Pottersfield Prize competition. I have profited greatly from our friendship.

Lesley Choyce, Peggy Amirault, and Julia Swan, I deeply appreciate your hard work on behalf of my book.

Anita Lahey and Una McDonnell, I'm indebted to both of you for your compassion, love, and friendship. Who knew all this would happen when the late Diana Brebner allowed us into her little tribe some twenty-one years ago.

Love to Sheila and David Buxton for being generous and kind grandparents and Margaret Elizabeth Buxton for being the perfect Auntie.

Shauna McKenna – we would never have survived without you. Thank you.

Alwynne Ling and Merise Brebner, thank you for all your love and kindness towards India.

Thank you, Yolly, for your care and the Chicken Adobo.

If it had not been for the intelligence, kindness, and unwavering support of my amazing husband Mark Leslie Taylor I might not have ever been able to finish this book. This memoir demanded a great deal from both of us. Thank you for being part of its creation.

To my India: Everywhere I go, you go with me.